JOBS FOR LAWYERS

JOBS FOR LAWYERS

Effective Techniques for Getting Hired in Today's Legal Marketplace

Hillary Jane Mantis
Kathleen Brady

IMPACT PUBLICATIONS
Manassas Park, VA

Library of Congress Cataloging-in-Publication Data

Mantis, Hillary Jane, 1960 -
    Jobs for lawyers: effective techniques for getting hired in
today's legal marketplace / Hillary Jane Mantis, Kathleen Brady.
      p.   cm.
    Includes bibliographical references and index.
    ISBN 1-57023-054-4 (alk. paper)
    1. Lawyers—United States—Marketing. 2. Lawyers—Vocational
guidance—United States. I. Brady, Kathleen, 1961 - .
KF316.5.M36 1995
340'.023'73—dc20   95-38917
                                                  CIP

For information on distribution or quantity discount rates, Tel. 703/361-7300, Fax 703/335-9486, or write to: Sales Department, IMPACT PUBLICATIONS, 9104-N Manassas Drive, Manassas Park, VA 22111-5211. Distributed to the trade by National Book Network, 4720 Boston Way, Suite A, Lanham, MD 20706, Tel. 301/459-8696 or 800/462-6420.

CONTENTS

Dedication

To Florence Goodzeit, my 7th grade English teacher, who was the first person to suggest that I might someday be a writer.

—Kathleen Brady

To my parents, for their support and encouragement.

—Hillary J. Mantis

ACKNOWLEDGMENTS

In keeping with the Academy Awards "30 second rule," we decided it would be impossible to thank everyone individually who contributed in some fashion to this book without going on for pages and pages. We simply would like to collectively thank our families and friends for their love and support over the years as well as our NALP colleagues for their willingness to share their wisdom and insights.

With that said, however, a few people do warrant special recognition for their assistance with the researching, typing and editing of this publication: Bernadette Dormer, Joanne Brady and David McGetrick. We also extend a note of thanks to Howard Libov for his advice and counsel regarding the world of publishing.

A very special thank you goes to our mentors, from whom we have learned so much about our professional selves:

Suzanne Baer, Diversity Consultant, Association of the Bar of the City of NY
John D. Feerick, Dean of Fordham University School of Law
Carol Kanarek, Kanarek and Shaw
Maureen Provost-Ryan, Assistant Dean, St. John's University School of Law
Robert J. Reilly, Assistant Dean, Fordham University School of Law
Carol Vecchio, Centerpoint

JOBS FOR LAWYERS

1

MASTERING THE LEGAL JOB MARKET OF THE 1990's

Approximately 250,000 new lawyers entered the legal profession in the 1980's. As the economy expanded so did the number of rich clients. Salaries skyrocketed accordingly. However, with the 1990's came the recession and a radical revision of the way business is done in the United States.

The practice of law has changed. No longer is lawyering a genteel profession. Today, competition for business is fierce as clients shop around for the best deal. Capital is enormous. New technology has created the need for instant answers. These changes have prompted law firms to become more like businesses, government agencies to scale back and public service organizations' doors to close.

With over 720,000 lawyers practicing in the United States, and approximately 40,000 new bar admissions each year, the profession is growing at the rate of about 25,000 lawyers per year. Contrast that with 1994 figures which indicate that the nation's largest law firms grew by an average of just 0.8%. Given these figures, it is obvious that individuals will have to learn how to remain marketable **throughout** their careers.

Today's lawyers must become "informed consumers." Lawyers will have to become more aware of impending changes in the legal marketplace and more adaptable to transformations. By doing so, lawyers can stay one step ahead of the changes and remain marketable in a highly unpredictable job market.

TRENDS IN TODAY'S LEGAL MARKETPLACE

What changes are we likely to see in the years to come in the legal job market? Here are some predictions:

1. **Large firms will continue to shrink in size or remain stable; hiring will be cautious**. Attorneys in large firms will have to make sure they do not become "slotted" in one area or on one case for too long; otherwise they will lose some degree of marketability. It will become more important to develop varied skills and rainmaking ability than to just have a large prestigious firm name on a resume.

2. **Expect a lot of growth opportunities with small law firms in the 1990's, especially with boutique practices.** Small law firms are developing very sophisticated practices. For example, boutique firms are opening in specialized areas such as intellectual property and environmental law. Many senior associates who do not make partner at large law firms will start small high quality law firms or become solo practitioners.

3. **In-house counsel positions will continue to increase, especially in smaller (fewer than 500 employee) companies**. In-house counsel positions continue to be a very popular option for mid-senior level attorneys. Only 12% of new hires came directly from law school in 1994, according to the National Association for Law Placement.

4. **Geographic flexibility will become more and more important with shifts in industry.** The east coast continues to be a declining source of opportunity. Attorneys may have to relocate several times during their careers to follow growth opportunities.

> ### Cities with the Lowest Unemployment Rate
>
> According to Bernard Haldane Associates, as of June 1994 the cities with the lowest unemployment rate included:
>
> Lincoln, Nebraska
> Madison, Wisconsin
> Santa Fe, New Mexico
> Raleigh Durham, North Carolina
> Stamford/Norwalk, Connecticut
> Tuscon, Arizona
> Des Moines, Iowa
> Minneapolis/St. Paul, Minnesota
> Honolulu, Hawaii

5. **The traditional titles of partner and associate will change.** We are likely to see new categories created for experienced, non-equity partners. Titles such as contract attorney, of counsel, and staff attorney will be introduced. Additionally, contract, temporary, per diem and consulting work will continue to grow as law firms continue to look at the bottom line costs of hiring full-time associates.

6. **Traditional law firm and corporate structure will continue to change** from a traditional pyramid-like leveraged structure, bottom heavy with associates, to a new more balanced structure with fewer entry level associates at the bottom, and a reduced associate-partner ratio. This will continue to result in an increase in **lateral** hiring and a decrease in **entry-level hiring.** However, firms are cautiously optimistic about business returning, and are hiring entry-level associates, but in smaller numbers.

7. **Part-time and temporary work are options that will grow for attorneys.** While the Bureau of Labor Statistics reports that about 16% of those employed in professional specialties during 1993 were working part time schedules, the National Association for Law Placement reports that only 2.4% of the attorneys represented in their 1994 *Directory of Legal Employers* work part-time, despite the fact that 86% of the nearly 1000 law offices represented in the directory indicated that they allow part-time schedules.

8. **Networking, rainmaking and marketing skills for attorneys to promote themselves and develop a client base will become increasingly crucial** for attorneys at all levels, both partner and associate. Attorneys will need to develop and hone these skills throughout their careers.

9. **Changes in political administrations will create new and challenging job opportunities.** As we swing back and forth between Democratic and Republican controlled Administrations, watch for changes and opportunities in the federal government, as well as on the Hill.

10. **Flexible schedules, alternative work arrangements, vacation time and sabbaticals and continuing educational opportunities will become more important, and highly valued** as opportunities to quickly move up the ladder remain limited.

HOT LEGAL PRACTICES

The following areas of practice are becoming hot in today's legal job marketplace:

- **Health Care**: The proposed far-reaching government reforms to the current health care system, coupled with health care emerging as one the fastest growing service industries, has created work for lawyers, both in the government and the private sector.

- **Elder Law**: The increased aging population, caused by high birthrates in the pre-depression era, and advanced medical technologies which enable people to live longer, has provided many opportunities for lawyers in the area of trusts and estate management, as well as addressing other legal concerns of the elderly.

- **Intellectual Property**: State of the art technology in the computer and biotechnology fields has created ongoing work for attorneys who deal in patents, trademarks, copyrights and trade secrets. Patent litigation is expected to continue to be a booming area, as companies are forced to defend their innovations.

- **Environmental Law**: Environmental law continues to be a hot area for lawyers in the 90's, as government legislation containing environmental provisions provokes disputes; thus the need for litigation, as well as interpretation. Watch for upcoming legislation affecting Superfund and the Clean Water Act.

- **Alternative Dispute Resolution:** The overcrowded court system has resulted in more parties turning to arbitration or mediation as a means to quickly resolve disputes.

- **Labor Law**: Especially in the area of employment discrimination, and sexual harassment claims, labor law is a growing field.

- **International Law and International Trade Regulation**: With an increase in investments abroad resulting in part from the passage of N.A.F.T.A. and other legislation, international transaction work and related litigation is at an all time high—but watch for changes in legislation.

- **Other Hot Areas**: Other areas predicted to create work for lawyers include a resurgence in some areas of finance, corporate and real estate.

INCREASED SERVICES TO THE LEGAL INDUSTRY

As lawyers adapt to the new computer technology, hi-tech service industries for lawyers are mushrooming. At the 1994 American Bar

Association Annual Meeting Expo Center, there were more exhibitors in the computer hardware/software category than in any other area. The exhibition offered CD-ROM programs, databases, case management software, video conferencing, support staff programs, on-line services and legal tech periodicals. Many of the representatives of these enterprises are former attorneys themselves, who have created a mini-industry.

So what does all this mean for attorneys engaged in a job search? In order to thrive in this market, lawyers need to adjust to these new rules and learn the techniques of job hunting.

It is important to understand that opportunities **are** available, even in a depressed market, for those who understand how and where they fit into the world of work and how the job market operates.

TEST YOUR MARKETABILITY

As you prepare to enter the legal job market, ask yourself these questions:

1. Do you have a **client base** and how diversified is it?
2. Are you knowledgeable in **more than one** area of the law?
3. Have you sent out your resume in the past year to **road test your marketability?** Is your resume up to date?
4. Are you keeping up with **political trends** to see how upcoming legislation and elections could affect your practice?
5. Are you watching market projections to be aware of where the next **hot practice area** will be?
6. Is the area of the country that you live in **growing**, with expanded sources for opportunity?

2

UNDERSTANDING THE JOB SEARCH PROCESS

Most lawyers think of the job search as a linear process—respond to ads by drafting resumes and cover letters, interview for positions and then consider offers. However, the process is actually circular. The job search process consists of four major steps as outlined on page 10. Completion of each step moves you further toward reaching your goal—finding a satisfying and rewarding job.

CAREER DEVELOPMENT PROCESS

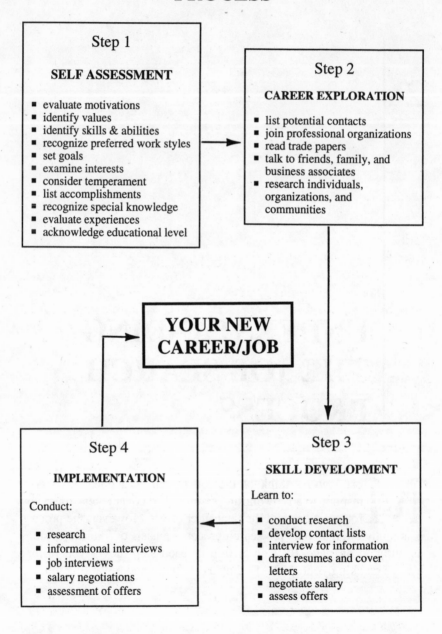

Step 1

SELF ASSESSMENT

- evaluate motivations
- identify values
- identify skills & abilities
- recognize preferred work styles
- set goals
- examine interests
- consider temperament
- list accomplishments
- recognize special knowledge
- evaluate experiences
- acknowledge educational level

Step 2

CAREER EXPLORATION

- list potential contacts
- join professional organizations
- read trade papers
- talk to friends, family, and business associates
- research individuals, organizations, and communities

YOUR NEW CAREER/JOB

Step 4

IMPLEMENTATION

Conduct:

- research
- informational interviews
- job interviews
- salary negotiations
- assessment of offers

Step 3

SKILL DEVELOPMENT

Learn to:

- conduct research
- develop contact lists
- interview for information
- draft resumes and cover letters
- negotiate salary
- assess offers

EFFECTIVE JOB SEARCH METHODS

- 10-11% of job seekers get positions through the use of search consultants

- 10-11% of job seekers get positions by answering advertisements in the newspapers or law school alumni career planning newsletters and through direct mail to target employers

- 80% of job seekers get their job through **networking**

USE YOUR TIME ACCORDINGLY!

THE JOB SEARCH

The job market, which is conservative and myopic by nature, requires a great deal of understanding and hard work by the job seeker in order to land a job. Employers interpret your capabilities in terms of your past career choices and your tenure in prior settings. Understandably, your most recent position is the clearest indication of your highest level of competency. The fact that you are making a change can raise questions about your motives. Are you running toward something or away from something? It is important to stay in control of your search to ensure that these market forces do not dictate your choices. Job seekers must use all the resources available to them to customize an approach to suit individual needs and overcome market obstacles.

Every job search book on the market expresses a resounding theme: **do what you do best and do what makes you happy**. Just finding any job is not enough. It is important to find a job that energizes you, involves skills which come naturally to you and is situated in a setting you find compatible. By taking the time to understand where you fit in the world of work and to learn successful job hunting techniques, you are likely to thrive in this competitive market.

EFFECTIVE METHODS

Typically, when people enter the job market, the first thing they do is survey the Classified Ads section of the newspaper, despite the fact that studies show that no more than 15% of placements occur through such formal mechanisms. According to Richard Bolles, author of ***What Color is Your Parachute?,*** the average company hires one person for every 1,470 resumes it receives. Obviously, job seekers who rely solely on traditional search strategies, like scanning classified ads or going to executive recruiters, won't find work easily. Plan to use a variety of methods to approach the market in proportion to their effectiveness.

Informal and personal methods of filling vacancies are preferred by both employers and employees over more formal mechanisms because informal methods are more in-depth and accurate. Employers are much more likely to hire an individual they know and can rely upon or someone who is known by an individual they respect. Employers are not anxious to have to process hundreds of resumes and applications that flood in when an ad is placed in the newspaper. Informal methods are also preferred because they reduce recruiting costs and hiring risks.

It is paradoxical that attorneys, who are so adept at massive research projects, ignore the research stage of the job search process. Most attorneys skip **Step 1—Self-Assessment, Step 2—Career Exploration**, and **Step 3—Skill Development** and instead begin at the end with **Step 4—Implementation**. The same people who would never think of going to court or to a meeting unprepared short-change themselves in the job search process by not being properly prepared.

USE A BUSINESS PLAN APPROACH

A job hunt does not have to be a devastating experience; it does not take guts so much as it requires thought, stamina and a willingness to sacrifice monetary pleasures for a long term goal. Keep in mind that job searches take a long time. Legal Search Consultants suggest that people should expect to be in the process one month for every $10,000 they earn. A creative job search may take longer.

Given the nature of today's economy, a proactive, creative approach to your job search is essential. Therefore, before you pick up the Classified Ads Section, consider using a "Business Plan" Approach. By following the steps outlined in this book, you will be able to successfully:

- **define** your "product" (through self-assessment)
- **analyze** your market (through career exploration)
- **market** your product (through your resume and cover letters)
- **sell** your product (by translating skills and assets into benefits)
- **evaluate** your offers

Make sure you do not spend too much time on process and not enough time on some of the more challenging activities such as self-assessment, networking and interviewing. Remember, it is not necessarily the most qualified person who gets the job, rather, it is the person most skilled at finding a job.

START-UP JOB SEARCH TIPS

If you are conducting a job search while employed, avoid placing your current position in jeopardy.

- Do not tell colleagues of your plans prematurely.
- Do not use office equipment to facilitate your search.
- Schedule interviews wisely. Try to use personal/vacation days when possible. Too many doctors appointments and sick grandmothers will raise suspicions.
- Instruct potential employers not to contact you at the office. Include a sentence in your cover letters such as: "As I am currently working, I would appreciate a confidential call to my home number."
- Do not burn bridges. When you are ready to tell your employer you are leaving, develop a mutually comfortable exit.

3

CREATING A
PLAN OF ACTION

Whether you are in a job search voluntarily or involuntarily, you are no doubt asking yourself questions like:

- Is there some way to combine my practice with my other, equally important interests?
- Are there jobs available at my level and salary expectations or will I have to settle for less?
- Should I give up the practice of law altogether, and if so, what else can I do?

These questions can be overwhelming because there are no immediate answers. People get stymied and either opt to stay stuck in an unhappy situation or simply avoid the questions altogether. Playing it safe and staying in a position you have outgrown can actually damage your career. Most people end up happier after a transition but do not pursue it until they are forced to do so. Even knowing that there is light at the end of the tunnel, many job seekers are stymied by the darkness that must be endured to get there.

ASSESS WHERE YOU ARE GOING

Take a minute or two to read the exercise below. Place a check next to the statements that apply to you. (If you are employed, base your answers on your current job; if you are not employed, base your responses on your last job or on the types of positions for which you are applying.)

Your Job:

___ A. energizes rather than exhausts you.

___ B. engrosses you to the extent that you lose track of time.

___ C. involves skills that have always come naturally to you (for instance, writing and researching, public speaking, organization, attention to detail).

___ D. is situated in a setting that you find comfortable (do you prefer a large urban environment over a small town? a formal setting in an office building over a casual setting where the lawyers wear jeans to work?)

___ E. capitalizes on your natural strengths, not your weaknesses.

___ F. involves the degree of human interaction that you find most comfortable (do you want a job where you are on the phone for most of the day? in court? do you prefer a job where you primarily research cases in the law library?)

___ G. is something that you settled for rather than something you secretly hoped for.

___ H. is something that you feel you **should** do, or something you feel you **should** like.

___ I. forces you to act in a way that is highly unnatural to you (for instance, do not take a job that calls for hours of library research if you are the type of person who hates to sit still).

___ J. fulfills your parents' or spouse's expectations, not your own.

___ K. makes you somewhat depressed at the thought of working there before you even start the job.

___ L. is something you accepted hastily without thinking about it.

If you checked off three or more from A through F, you are on the right track. If you checked three or more from G through L, re-evaluate your career goals.

Many times job seekers start each morning declaring "Today I will find a new job!" This is a sure fire way to set yourself up for failure. You have to be willing to do your due diligence (or discovery for you litigators). By breaking the job search process down into small, manageable steps, you will avoid feeling overwhelmed and subsequently paralyzed.

TIPS TO GET YOU STARTED

TIP 1:   Address Negative Preconceptions

Many attorneys, searching for a logical reason for their predicament, create barriers for themselves by accepting perceived deficiencies about themselves. Recent graduates accept that they will not be hired because they have "no experience;" women and attorneys of color retreat because they feel employers "aren't really serious about hiring us" while more senior lawyers feel discriminated against because of their age and salary range. Just about every group has some reason to feel disenfranchised by the job market. Unfortunately, all of these perceptions create obstacles. However, they should not be viewed as insurmountable, but rather only inconvenient. It is up to you as the job seeker to test these erroneous perceptions and convince employers that you are the best person for the job. Keep in mind, if you do not believe you are the best person for the job, you will have a difficult time convincing any employer. Employers often declare their intent to hire "only the best and the brightest!" But when pressed to articulate what that means, recruiters struggle to offer a more precise explanation. The traditional definition of top 10 law school, top grades, law review and "big firm experience" is the most commonly cited criteria, perhaps because it is the most easily understood.

HOW TO SABOTAGE YOUR JOB SEARCH

- Think of yourself as average, unable to offer anything unique.

- Assume the rest of the world knows you are talented.

- Complain about past employers, present circumstances or the job search process.

- Neglect overwhelming emotional concerns.

- Let self-defeating behaviors (like being late for interviews, not following up with employers, sending carelessly prepared documents) characterize your job search.

- Neglect your personal appearance.

- Ignore personality traits (like talking too much or too little; a strong regional accent, poor posture, etc.) which may distract potential employers from identifying you as a strong candidate.

- Blindly accept preconceived notions as true.

Certain positive attributes are ascribed automatically to candidates possessing these qualifications whether or not they are truly deserved. The age old debate is, how real are these criteria? How good a set of predictors are they for determining success in a particular organization? How can job seekers who do not fit this profile succeed in a job search?

The legal hiring process seems to be based on these myopic preconceptions which may or may not be valid. Employers feel safer relying on "tried and true" methods to acquire the "best and brightest." Therefore, the burden falls on the job seeker to challenge these time honored preconceptions. Consider using your job search campaign to showcase your skills to recruiters. For example, a candidate who can articulate a keen understanding of the nature of a prospective employer's business via a well crafted cover letter can illustrate writing ability, research capabilities, and an ability to help an organization better service clients. Analogize how those same skills could be used to represent clients creatively, to disarm opposing counsel effectively and to represent the organization proudly. Through

OVERCOMING THE "GRADE" OBSTACLE

Grades **are** an important measure of one's intellectual ability. However, recent graduates would be wise to remind recruiters that a G.P.A. alone does not provide the whole story. It is extremely useful to underscore "patterns." For example, a transcript containing all A's and one D may show the same G.P.A. as one filled with all B's. It is probably worthwhile to note that distinction as well as grades that markedly improved during the second and third years of Law School. Similarly, you may have done extremely well in courses where the grade was based on a paper but not as well on timed exams. Could that distinction be important? These subtleties will be lost on recruiters who are rigid in their G.P.A. cutoffs and only look to the bottom line unless the job seeker does an adequate job of calling attention to them.

Most hiring officials agree, successful lawyers must be able to pull apart a legal problem, break it down to its logical components and analyze it. By highlighting courses taken as well as grades and honors received, job seekers illustrate their acumen in this area.

There are other intangible qualities lawyers need to possess in order to be successful. Things like maturity, stability, fortitude, congeniality, the ability to remain unruffled under pressure and to meet deadlines are keys to a flourishing legal career. These are things not easily measured by grades nor are they easily uncovered during the interview process. Job seekers would do well to provide employers with insights into these areas by highlighting things like:

- **clinical or pro bono experiences** demonstrating practical lawyering skills;
- **prior work experience** indicating "special knowledge" a candidate might possess;
- **extracurricular activities** illustrating leadership abilities;
- **family responsibilities** exemplifying the ability to balance many pressures successfully;
- **community involvement** indicating potential business development opportunities.

the process, an applicant's level of maturity and self-confidence can be easily spotted as well as their ability for creative problem solving and designing alternative, effective methods to achieve their goals. Suggest to employers that given that the workplace and client base are changing so dramatically these days, organizational survival may depend on its workforce's proficiency in such skills.

Similarly, job seekers who can spot a market need, articulate their ability to fill it and challenge employers to test their preconceptions about "successful" candidates will have demonstrated the intangible qualities so often sought by employers.

TIP 2:   Allocate a Specific Amount of Time

To get started, you must decide how much time you can realistically devote to your search. If you are currently working, consider 2-3 hours per week; if you are unemployed, consider 6-8 hours a day. Maintaining a steady and consistent effort throughout your search will be one of the most important elements in determining your success. A "start and stop" approach almost always leads you back to square one at each juncture. Working in bursts of activity will ensure failure. You must use the same degree of diligence for your job search as you do for projects at work.

TIP 3:   Adhere to a Schedule

Regardless of how many hours you have allocated to the process, work out a schedule and make a personal commitment to stick to it. During those reserved hours, your job search must be your primary focus. This is the time committed to self-assessment exercises, making job related phone calls, conducting library research, etc. Do not allow yourself to be interrupted by running errands, baby sitting, etc. By adhering to a schedule, you will reduce the insecurity most job seekers feel about their situations because you will be in control. You will also be able to chart your progress.

TIP 4:   Select a System to Record Your Activities

Whether you opt for a notebook and pen or an elaborate

computer based system, you must develop a system for record-ing your activities in order to easily retrieve important data and to ensure appropriate follow-up actions. You may want to visit an office products or discount store to give you some ideas about what kind of system will work best for you.

TIP 5:   Consider Your Finances

How much money do you **need** to earn in order to maintain your current lifestyle? Just because a $30,000 a year legal services job may be out of the question does not mean that a $150,000 a year large firm position is the only alternative. There are a substantial number of legal, legally related and non-legal positions that pay very acceptable salaries. Before seeking a new position, write out a detailed budget for yourself and your family. This preliminary investigation into salary will help you later on as you approach salary negotiations.

TIP 6:   Be Discreet!

In order to protect your current position while conducting a job search, observe a few simple standards of discretion.

- Do not tell your colleagues about your search. Even trusted friends sometimes gossip and you do not want your employer to learn of your search prematurely.
- Do not use office equipment to facilitate your search.
- Try to use personal/vacation days to interview. Employ-ers tend to notice people leaving early or late too often or those who have an inordinate amount of doctors appointments and deaths in the family.

SAMPLE ACTIVITY SHEET

Target Employer (name, address, phone)	Primary Contact	Date Contacted	Follow-up action required	End Results	Additional Info

TIP 7:   Call the Career Services Office of Your Law School

Many law graduates, even recent ones, are unaware that they can schedule individual appointments for career counseling with a counselor at their law school's office of career services. An initial appointment with a career counselor (generally free of charge) can provide valuable information, ideas, and a direction in which to start your career search.

Most schools are not equipped to offer long-term counseling, however, you ought to go learn more about the services your school offers its alumni. Most schools will provide resume and cover letter advisement, in person or by fax, enabling graduates who no longer live in the area to use the service. Many offices provide interview skills seminars, mock interviews and job search support groups. Nearly every law school has created a newsletter, published either monthly or bi-monthly and mailed to graduates, containing job listings of lateral positions. Job newsletters can offer a wealth of information and possible job leads because many schools receive listings from their alumni which are not published elsewhere. A number of law schools also trade their newsletter with other schools thus enabling their graduates access to job listings from schools located in different geographic areas.

To accommodate a graduate seeking employment in another geographic area, most law schools are able to arrange reciprocity for their graduates in that area for a limited duration (usually three months). Otherwise, a non-graduate of the school will generally be prohibited from using that school's career center. If granted reciprocity, the graduate will usually have access to most of the resources that the school offers its own graduates. In recent more competitive times, however, some schools have curtailed reciprocity, reserving all services for their own graduates.

Every law school's Office of Career Services contains a mini library for graduates to research job opportunities, jot down listings, and read directories, books and periodicals relevant to the job search. By utilizing your career library, you can save a lot of expensive subscription costs and have access to a multitude of resources. Many graduates do not realize that law school career services offices spend a lot of time compiling their own resources which they give to their students and graduates. Most schools put together and distribute lists of state and regional law firms and in-house corporate legal departments. Law schools often have many handouts relating to different steps in the job search, including resume/cover letter guides and other valuable information.

In light of recent advances in technology, law schools have also been able to upgrade their resource libraries and offer many computerized on-line services. Perhaps the most import-ant advance in recent years has been the arrival of the Martindale-Hubbell directory on Lexis and NALPLine and West's Legal Directory on Westlaw. Both databases enable the user to manipulate the directories to create a narrowly targeted mailing list. For example, on Lexis you can request a list of personal injury firms with two to twelve attorneys practicing in New York City, and the computer will generate this list from Martindale-Hubbell. You can further narrow the list by requesting firms with alumni from your own alma mater. NALPLine on Westlaw can be used in a similar manner, and also contains salary, recruitment and other information com-piled by the National Association for Law Placement. Call their customer service representatives to ask for handouts on how to effectively use their services. (Lexis/Nexis: 1-800-543-6862; Westlaw: 1-800-937-8529).

TIP 8:   Call Your Local Bar Association

State and local bar associations have done a commendable job supplementing the work of the law schools in offering support groups, workshops and seminars for their membership. The Association of the Bar of the City of New York, for example, has a "Lawyers in Transition" Committee that offers numerous seminars featuring career experts and on-going weekly support groups run by psychologists. It also offers job bulletins to its members. Although the wealth of new programs offered may not solve the economic crisis, it has vastly increased net-working opportunities and provided much-needed emotional support.

TIP 9:   Allow Yourself Some Playtime

Whether you are in the job search voluntarily or involuntarily, there is a tendency to avoid other people. Job seekers feel guilty if every waking moment is not dedicated to their search. Because there is rejection built into the job search process, it is important to design strategies for working through the rejection so that you have the energy to move on to the next call or meeting or interview which may be the one where you land a job. Allow yourself time to be with the important people in your life who can provide support, encouragement and perhaps a few laughs during this tumultuous time.

CONSIDER YOUR OPTIONS

In order to help you establish the focus of your job search, lawyers in transition ought to decide whether they wish to consider opportunities in different practice settings or areas of practice.

Different Practice Settings

Although this may seem obvious, switching practice settings has made a world of difference for many attorneys. It is also the least drastic, and easiest change to make. Choices include:

- Move from the private sector to the public sector or vice-versa.
- Move from a large firm to a small firm.
- Move from an urban environment to a suburban environment, or from a firm's main office to a branch office.
- Move to a different environment while utilizing the same skills; i.e., from insurance defense litigation in a law firm to a similar position in an insurance company.
- Change to a firm with different types of clients.

A good way to deal with this issue is to take an inventory of your most desired work settings and options.

Complete the following checklist by indicating which options most interest you:

A. Law Firm
___Solo Practice
___2 - 10 Attorneys
___11 - 25 Attorneys
___26 - 50 Attorneys

___51 - 100 Attorneys
___101 - 250 Attorneys
___251 - 500 Attorneys
___500 + Attorneys

Representing

___Businesses
___Businesses with significant pro bono opportunities
___Businesses and individuals
___Individuals (___defense/___plaintiff)
___Individuals (non-litigation)
___Public Interest
___Other (specify)_____

B. Government

Federal

___Executive
___Legislative
___Judicial (__trial/__appellate)
___US Attorney
___Armed Forces

State

___Executive
___Legislative
___Judicial (__trial/__appellate)
___Attorney General

County or Regional

___Executive
___Legislative
___Judicial (__trial/__appellate)
___District Attorney

Municipal

___Executive
___Legislative
___Judicial (__trial/__appellate)
___City Solicitor

C. Academic

___Law School Professor
___Law School Administrator
___Other School Professor
___Other School Administrator
___Librarian

D. Public Interest/Human Services

___Legal Services Programs
___Individual Representation
___Class Action, Law Reform
___Policy, Research
___Litigation
___Public Defender
    (__Trials/__Appeals)

___Public Interest Law Centers
___Individual Representation
___Class Action, Law Reform
___Policy, Research
___Litigation
___Social Action Organizations
___Citizen/Community Organizations
___Nonprofit Organizations

E. Corporation In-house Counsel (Profit/Non-Profit)

___Business
___Non-Profit
___Hospital/Health Organization
___Banking/Financial Services
___Real Estate Development
___Insurance
___Accounting
___Management Consulting

___Foundation
___Labor Union
___Trade Association
___College and University
___Museum
___Professional Society
___Religious Organization

F. Other

___Delivery of Legal Services   ___Elective Politics
    Systems   ___Legal Clinics
___Pre-Paid Legal Services   ___Non-traditional legal career
___Private Foundations

Different Practice Areas

Many attorneys are upset to discover that, having chosen the real estate department as a first year associate, they are forever condemned to practice real estate law. Moving to a different area of practice involves a substantive change, which can be much more difficult to make than moving to a different practice setting. Here are some good ways to start:

- Attend continuing legal education courses offered by the American Bar Association, state and local bar associations, Law Institutes, and private companies.

- Join the relevant section of the American Bar Association and your state or local bar association. Membership often includes a subscription to a publication that provides information on new developments in the field and upcoming programs. Volunteer to work as an active member. This will provide excellent opportunities for networking and learning about the subject, as well as establishing credibility.

- Take courses at a local university related to your area of interest. You do not have to commit to getting a degree. Many schools have certificate or "visiting professional" programs.

- Enroll in an LL.M. program.

- Do volunteer work for an organization in your area of interest.

- If you want to remain with the same employer but in a different area of practice, talk to the head of the department you would like to work in and ask for an opportunity to work on a case in that area. Try to bring in a client in the area you want to work in and ask to co-counsel the case. Bolster your credibility by availing yourself of the aforementioned courses.

Consider the variety of practice areas in which you can work. Underline the ones which are of interest to you:

Alternate Dispute Resolution

Mediation
Negotiation
Arbitration

Art, Entertainment and Media

Motion Pictures
Sports
Music
Computer Art/Graphics
Press
TV and Radio
Cable television

Art and Theater
Recreation/Leisure
Communication
Culture
Libel
Literary Property
First Amendment
Video

Business Law

Banking
Corporations
Securities Regulation
Bankruptcy
Corporate Finance
Admiralty & Maritime
Energy
Investment Banking
Utilities
Industrial
Reorganization
Mergers

Commodities
Trade Regulation
Unfair Competition
Oil & Gas
Mining
Natural Resources
Advertising
Insurance
Foreign Trade
Economic Development
Interstate Commerce
Agriculture

Civil Litigation

Appellate Litigation
Practice and Procedure before

Administrative Agencies
Malpractice

Personal Injury
  and Negligence

Trial Practice and Procedure
Products Liability

Consumer Goods and Services

General Purchasing
Debtor's Rights
Insurance
Transportation
Product Liability

Energy
Food
Corporate Responsibility
Utilities
Pharmaceuticals

Criminal Justice

Criminal Law Trial
Criminal Law Appeals
Prisoner's Rights

Probation and Parole
Juvenile Justice
Rehabilitation

Employment

Worker Safety
Equal Employment
Collective Bargaining
Pension/ERISA
Worker's Compensation

Employee Benefits
Civil Service
Labor (Management)
Labor (Union)
Unemployment

Family Law

Adoption
Conservatorship
Foster Parenting
Wills, Trusts
Marriage
Divorce

Guardianship
Settlement of Estates
Parent Custody Rights
Children's Rights
Surrogate Parenting
Neglect and Abuse

Health

Physical Health
Disabled Persons
Abused Persons
Mental Health

AIDS
Health Care Systems
Commitment

Law Practice

Law Office Economics
Paralegal Services
Prepaid Legal Services
Professional Education
Specialization
Law Research Materials

Advertising
Ethics
Legal Clinics
General Practice
Recruitment
Management

Property Law and Real Estate

Architecture
Construction
Conveyancing
Cooperative
Building Codes
Condemnation
Condominiums

Eminent Domain
Environmental Law
Land Use
Shopping Centers
Tenant Rights
Urban Development

Public Interest/Human Services

International Human Rights
Civil Rights
Civil Liberties
Women's Rights
Elder Law
Minority Rights
Community Organizing/
   Citizen Action
Municipal Affairs
Education

Legislation
Election
Youth
Urban Affairs
Welfare
Rural Residents
Small Farm Owners
Military Justice
Veterans
Immigration

Antitrust
Poverty
Constitutional
Government

Disarmament/
  Arms Control
Environment
Disability Law

Science and Technology

Aeronautics
Engineering
Genetics
Patent

Copyright
Trademark
Computers

Taxation

Income and Other Taxation
Estate and Gift Taxation

Practice and Administration
Federal and State Liaison

As you explore your options, keep three simple rules in mind:

1. Always trust your own instincts.
2. Try not to let money completely rule your life.
3. Motivate yourself.

4

DEFINING YOUR PRODUCT: SELF-ASSESSMENT FOR LAWYERS

Ideally, work is supposed to be fun. However, if you are looking for a job right now, fun may be the furthest thing from your mind. Any job opening may seem like a good prospect to you now. Even if you are employed, you may feel "stuck" in your job and ready to jump at the first opportunity.

Accepting a long-term/permanent position out of desperation, however, can lead you back to the same rut you were in. Too often candidates feel at the mercy of a bad job market and believe that job satisfaction is a luxury. Granted, making a career change can be difficult—but if you are in the market for a job, you also have the opportunity to find something that you like much better than your previous job. Whether you are looking for your first or your fifth legal position, do not short-change yourself. Take some time to think about what you really want. Your focus should be inward, with the purpose being to figure out how you would like to spend your career without being limited by what you think you could get employed to do. The paradox of a job search is that you must be focused, yet open to the possibilities at the same time. Think beyond your current field from the outset, not only after you have experienced difficulty in your search.

EXPLORING YOUR PERSONAL STYLE, MOTIVES, VALUES AND SKILLS

It is important to be able to **articulate** your strengths, passions, preferred work style, goals, enthusiasms, values, contributions, potential, ideals, interest areas, temperament, accomplishments, special knowledge and motivations. It is equally important to be aware of your weaknesses so that you can minimize them. Try to think like a Madison Avenue advertiser. For example, if you were trying to sell a toothpaste that when used regularly prevented cavities and tasted awful, your commercial would not start out "Brand X tastes really awful, but you will never get a cavity!" The only thing your audience will remember is that your product does not taste good. By the same token, highlighting the fact that "although I have no litigation experience, I have..." emphasizes your weakness! **You must always play to your strengths in the job search process.**

Lawyers are naturally proficient in the analysis and synthesis of data. And what better subject to research than yourself? Self-assessment is the key to any successful career, yet most lawyers fail to do it. At best, they can assess their **lifestyles**—where and how they want to live, what their immediate needs are, and what their needs are likely to be tomorrow. These are certainly important considerations, but evaluating lifestyles is no substitution for self-assessment.

The process of self-assessment will afford you the opportunity to:

- Clarify your objectives
- Articulate your goals
- Describe and market yourself to potential employers
- Evaluate employment options
- Take charge of your future

You survived the first year of law school; you survived the bar examination; surely you can survive the equally challenging experience of self-assessment. It will take time and effort to recall the experiences you have had throughout your lifetime and categorize them into those which have frustrated you, challenged you, brought you happiness, etc., but it will be time well spent.

Personal Style

Career theorist John Holland developed a theory base on the assumption that there are six types of people and six types of jobs—**Realistic, Investigative, Artistic, Social, Enterprising** and **Conventional.** He hypothesized that people are naturally drawn to jobs in which they can be themselves, playing to their strengths, surrounded by people like themselves.

Discovery of your type allows you to understand who you really are —at the core. It describes how you function when you are most relaxed, operating in the world without effort, and under no pressure.

These six types also can be extended to the legal profession. Different types of people are naturally drawn to different types of practice. Consider the following types.

TYPE	STYLE	POSSIBLE PRACTICE SETTINGS
REALISTIC	Prefers to deal with things more than ideas or people. Prefers concrete vs. abstract work tasks. Basically less sociable with structured thought pattern.	Regulatory Affairs Contract Review Environmental
INVESTIGATIVE	Intellectual, abstract, analytical, independent, sometimes radical and task oriented.	Litigation Judicial Clerk Law Secretary
ARTISTIC	Imaginative, independent and extroverted. Values aesthetics, and prefers self-expression through the art.	Entertainment Law Trademark/copyright

SOCIAL	Prefers social interaction, social presence, concerned with social problems, religious, community service oriented, and interested in educational activities.	Advocacy Public Defender Government Service Trust and Estates Family Law
ENTERPRISING	Extroverted, aggressive, adventurous, dominant, persuasive. Prefers leadership roles and makes use of good verbal skills.	Sole Practitioner Investment Banker Venture Capital Trial Lawyer
CONVENTIONAL	Practical, well-controlled, sociable, rather conservative. Prefers structured tasks and prefers conformity sanctioned by society.	Business Law In-house Corporate Counsel Government Service

See Chapter 4 for more information on self-assessment instruments.

Motives

Many of us spend more time planning our vacations than we do planning our careers. We are not clear about what is most important to us and arrive at decisions based not on reason, but based on feelings and intuitions.

Why did you decide to become an attorney? It seems like a simple enough question yet it is surprising that many attorneys cannot respond. People usually cite the customary, obligatory reasons like "to create a better society" or "to put my intellect to good use"; they tend to avoid the responses that they became lawyers for the money, or because of the glamour portrayed on TV and in the movies or simply because it was there. But keep in mind that goals change throughout careers. What moves you to action today may bore you and disillusion you tomorrow. Change should not be seen as a sign of weakness nor as a lack of commitment. Rather, change should be seen as a prerequisite to personal and professional growth.

Many times, obligations and justifications become overriding considerations in choosing career paths. For example, once the investment in law school has been made, there is enormous pressure to seek employment where one can earn the highest financial return—usually in the private sector. Goals of public service, politics or lawyering for the poor and unfortunate tend to wither as the reality sets in that efficiency and economics point in only one direction. To help you articulate your motives ask yourself:

- What are my priorities?
- What do I want from life? What am I after?
- What am I willing to sacrifice to achieve my goals?

People tend to be motivated by what they like, not by what makes sense. It is important to play to your "evil secrets"—those things that you might be embarrassed to say out loud but which really should be considered when evaluating career choices. To help you determine what motivates you, check the following "secret" job qualities you know in your heart you need to be happy:

____	Status
____	High Salary
____	Pension and other security benefits
____	Aesthetically pleasing physical working conditions
____	Being recognized and praised for good performance
____	Opportunity for self-development and improvement
____	Opportunity for advancement
____	Getting along with co-workers
____	Opportunity to do interesting work
____	Chance to turn out quality work
____	Ability to participate in the organization's decision making process
____	Close supervision and feedback
____	Responsibility over your work and that of others
____	To belong to a known and respected organization
____	To have an influence on others
____	To work for a cause/be of service
____	Ability to integrate other parts of life
____	To create something new
____	Sabbaticals to pursue activities outside of work

In addition, which of the following incentives is most important to you:

___ Security	___ Managerial Responsibilities
___ Organizational identity	___ Creativity
___ Autonomy	___ Sense of Service
___ Technical Ability	___ Intellectual Challenge
	___ Lifestyle Integration

Values

Values are those intangible principles and standards that bring meaning to your work and motivate your involvement and commitment. You need to ask yourself what your values are and which hold the most meaning and importance to you. People tend to feel most comfortable when surrounded by others who hold similar values and in situations where their values are appreciated. The following exercise will help you further identify career/work values and factors crucial to your job satisfaction.

Rate the importance of each item

A=Very Important   B= Important   C=Not Important

___Achievement
___Advancement
___Aesthetics
___Affiliation
___Altruism
___Authority & Power
___Autonomy
___Being Needed
___Boss You Respect
___Challenge
___Change
___Closure
___Commitment to Goal(s)
___Competition
___Complexity
___Control
___Courage
___Creativity
___Direct Impact
___Discovering New Things
___Diversity
___Economic Return
___Effectiveness
___Ethics
___Excellence
___Excitement & Adventure
___Fairness

___Flexibility
___Focus
___Harmony
___High Profile
___High Risk/High Reward
___Holistic Approach
___Improving the World
___Independence
___Individuality
___Influencing People
___Innovation
___Integrity
___Intellectual Stimulation
___Interesting Work
___Interpersonal Relationships
___Job Security
___Justice
___Leadership of Others
___Lifestyle Integration
___Mentoring
___Morality
___Originality
___Personal Growth
___Pleasant Surroundings
___Pleasure & Fun
___Pressure & Fast Pace
___Prestige

___Profit/Gain	___Social Relevance
___Public or Client Contact	___Specialization
___Recognition	___Stability
___Respect	___Status
___Responsibility	___Structured Environment
___Results of Work Seen	___Supervision
___Reward	___Supervision of Others
___Salary	___Training
___Security	___Traveling
___Self-Development	___Variety
___Self Expression	___Working Alone
___Service	___Working on Teams
___Simplicity	___Other_____

Review the values you ranked "A" and **order** these from 1 to 10 in order of importance to you. Keep in mind that like motives, values may shift as you mature and grow, but most guide your choices throughout a lifetime.

Skills

The best strategy for directing the course of your career is to focus on your skills. Jobs are joint ventures in problem solving. The idea is to find a match between an employer's needs and your skills. The basic questions in every career are:

- What needs to be done?
- What have you been learning?
- What can you **do**?

You can begin idenifying your skills by completing the following exercise:

Using adjectives, complete the sentence "I can ____" at least 20 times. When you complete this go back to each sentence, add the phrase "for instance," and provide an example.

The point of this exercise is to remind yourself of the things you can do, as well as to arm you with specific examples which can be used during the interview process. Review the following list of verbs to help you get started.

SKILL IDENTIFICATION
ACTION VERBS—WHAT YOU **DO**

accelerate	catalog	deliver	figure
accept	catch	demonstrate	file
accomplish	cause	describe	finance
account for	chair	design	focus
achieve	change	designate	forecast
acquire	check	detail	foresee
act	chose	determine	formulate
activate	classify	develop	forward
adapt	clear up	devise	foster
add	close	diagnosis	frame
adjust	coach	digest	gain
administer	combine	diminish	gather
advise	communicate	direct	generate
advocate	compare	discover	give
aid	complete	display	grab
alphabetize	compose	distill	grade
alter	conceive	draft	grasp
analyze	conceptualize	dramatize	greet
anticipate	conclude	draw	gross
apply	condition	earn	guide
appoint	conduct	educate	handle
appraise	confront	elect	hasten
approach	consolidate	elicit	heighten
arbitrate	construct	employ	help
argue	consult	encompass	highlight
arrange	continue	encourage	hike
articulate	contract	enjoy	hire
assess	control	enlarge	house
assist	convince	enlist	hunt
assume	coordinate	ensure	hypothesize
assure	copy	enter	identify
attend	correct	establish	illustrate
author	counsel	estimate	imagine
authorize	count	evaluate	implement
award	craft	excel	improve
balance	create	execute	improvise
begin	critique	exercise	include
bolster	dance	expand	incorporate
boost	deal	experiment	increase
brief	debate	explain	indicate
budget	decide	explore	inform
build	define	extrapolate	initiate
calculate	delegate	facilitate	innovate
care	delineate	familiarize	inspect

instruct	overcome	refine	study
insure	oversee	reflect	submit
interpret	pace	relate	suggest
interview	paint	remember	summarize
introduce	participate	renovate	supervise
investigate	perceive	repair	support
join	perform	report	surmount
joke	persist	represent	survey
judge	persuade	rescue	tailor
juggle	photograph	research	target
know	pioneer	respond	teach
labor	place	return	test
launch	plane	reveal	theorize
lead	play	review	think
learn	police	revise	tighten
lecture	position	save	tour
license	practice	scout	track
listen	prepare	screen	train
lobby	present	script	transcribe
locate	prevail	scrutinize	transfer
look	process	select	transform
maintain	produce	sell	translate
make	profit	sent	travel
manage	program	serve	treat
map out	prohibit	set	tutor
master	project	ship	type
maximize	promote	show	uncover
meet	prove	sift	understand
modify	publicize	simplify	undertake
monitor	publish	sing	unearth
motivate	purchase	solve	unfurl
move	qualify	sought	update
name	quantify	spearhead	utilize
neaten	quicken	specify	value
negotiate	quote	speechwriting	venture
net	rate	speaking	verbalize
notice	read	stage	view
nurture	realize	start	visualize
observe	receive	state	welcome
open	recognize	stop	win
operate	recommend	straighten	work
order	record	streamline	write
organize	recreate	strengthen	
originate	recruit	strip	

More specifically, think about the skills you may have with people, information and things. For example,

PEOPLE	INFORMATION	THINGS
Taking Instruction	Observing	Handling (Objects)
Serving	Comparing	Being Athletic
Sensing, Feeling	Copying, Storing	Working with Nature
Communicating	Retrieving	Working with Machines
Persuading	Computing	Using Tools
Performing	Researching	Operating Equipment
Managing	Analyzing	Operating Vehicles
Supervising	Organizing	Precision Working
Negotiating	Evaluating	Assembling Things
Deciding	Visualizing	Repairing
Founding, Leading	Improving, Adapting	Designing
Treating	Creating, Synthesizing	Expediting
Advising	Designing	
Consulting	Planning, Developing	
Counseling	Expediting	
Training	Achieving	

Qualities Needed for Success in the Practice of Law

The following traits are among those essential for the practice of Law. For each characteristic, on a scale from 1 to 5 (1=very little; 5=very strong) indicate the extent to which you believe you possess those qualities.

I am able to:_____.

For Example:_____.

Build networks	1 2 3 4 5
Analyze data	1 2 3 4 5
Assemble deals	1 2 3 4 5
Assimilate new data quickly	1 2 3 4 5
Be self-directed	1 2 3 4 5
Conceptualize	1 2 3 4 5
Conduct legal research	1 2 3 4 5
Counsel clients	1 2 3 4 5
Deal with people	1 2 3 4 5
Decide in pressure situations	1 2 3 4 5

Demonstrate commitment	1	2	3	4	5
Demonstrate good judgment/common sense	1	2	3	4	5
Demonstrate political judgment	1	2	3	4	5
Develop business	1	2	3	4	5
Develop rapport and trust	1	2	3	4	5
Digest large quantities of material	1	2	3	4	5
Draft documents	1	2	3	4	5
Empathize	1	2	3	4	5
Explain complicated ideas in simple terms	1	2	3	4	5
Follow through	1	2	3	4	5
Formulate strategy	1	2	3	4	5
Gather facts	1	2	3	4	5
Get along with colleagues	1	2	3	4	5
Inspire confidence	1	2	3	4	5
Interview	1	2	3	4	5
Keep confidences	1	2	3	4	5
Listen critically	1	2	3	4	5
Manage complex tasks	1	2	3	4	5
Manage people	1	2	3	4	5
Mediate	1	2	3	4	5
Negotiate	1	2	3	4	5
Organize	1	2	3	4	5
Produce	1	2	3	4	5
Put in long hours	1	2	3	4	5
Research	1	2	3	4	5
Retain information	1	2	3	4	5
Solve problems creatively	1	2	3	4	5
Speak persuasively	1	2	3	4	5
Summarize	1	2	3	4	5
Synthesize	1	2	3	4	5
Work well under pressure	1	2	3	4	5
Write persuasively	1	2	3	4	5

For each characteristic you ranked low, consider whether you can or want to develop this skill further.

IDENTIFYING YOUR SUCCESS PATTERN

Transferable/functional skills are ways that we characteristically react to problematic situations throughout life. As a child, if confronted with a puzzle or task, your reaction may have been to organize the pieces and then examine alternative solutions. As a teenager repairing a car engine, the same problem-solving skills may have been utilized. These problem-solving skills are known as "success patterns" and tend to become set during the teenage years. Over the years, we tend to become more proficient in the use of our favorite skills.

By reviewing past accomplishments—in any setting—you can easily identify success patterns. We all possess many skills; the question is which ones do we enjoy using most.

To help you focus on your favorite skills, try listing 20 achievements or accomplishments from throughout your lifetime, including those related to work, leisure and education. Remember, an accomplishment can be something very simple, like winning the spelling bee in the third grade or hosting your first successful dinner party or managing a personal crisis. Your skill patterns will emerge no matter which accomplishments you select. Try reviewing billing records, looking through yearbooks and family photo albums to help jog your memory.

Next, select two or three accomplishments on your list that you would like to examine more closely. Write a paragraph detailing every step you took to make this event happen. Concentrate on HOW you did it, but do not analyze. Have fun with this—do not worry about grammar, spelling or punctuation. At the end, note how you felt at the conclusion of the event. For example, you might write:

1. In the third grade I won the class spelling bee. The prize for the contest was a beautiful red bicycle. I told one of my classmates that I wanted to win the bike and he laughed and said "everyone knows you are the worst speller in the class." I knew he was right, but I also knew I had three weeks to prepare. I used our spelling work book and memorized each lesson. I also borrowed my fourth grad sister's spelling work book and studied those lessons too. For three weeks I gave up playing with my friends and watching TV. I just studied words constantly. Each night, my mother quizzed me on all the words. The day of the spelling bee I was confident. Finally, it was me and the smart alec who "challenged" me. When he misspelled "questionnaire" I knew that beautiful red bicycle was mine. I felt so happy and proud of myself.

2. In my junior year of college, I announced to my roommates that I was going to host a dinner party. Knowing my history in the kitchen, they laughed at me and bet me $100 that I could not cook and edible meal. I was determined to prepare a wonderful dinner, despite me prior misfortunes in the kitchen AND teach my roommates a lesson. I scoured through cookbooks in an attempt to find dishes which were elegant yet simple. Each night for weeks I practiced preparing different courses of the meal and solicited opinions of which were the best. At the same time I read through gourmet magazines to learn which flavors complement each other as well as to get ideas about

table arrangements, etc. One month later, I invited 8 of my friends (including my 2 roommates) to dinner. The table was beautiful...the food was delicious...and my roommates were $100 poorer. I was so pleased with my accomplishment.

From those examples, one might assume that the author is motivated by material rewards as well as by the sheer challenge. The author demonstrated discipline, determination, initiative and a willingness to sacrifice pleasure in order to achieve a goal. This information is important to know and easy to translate to employers during the interview process. "Ever since winning the third grade spelling bee, despite my poor spelling abilities, I have known that I am at my best when presented with a challenge.")

EXERCISE #1—Achievement Stories

Achievement 1: _____

_____

_____

_____

_____

Achievement 2: _____

_____

_____

_____

_____

_____

Achievement 3: _____

_____

_____

_____

_____

_____

Achievement 4: _____

_____

_____

_____

_____

_____

Achievement 5: _____

_____

_____

_____

_____

_____

Review your achievement paragraphs, circling all skills mentioned. Read the stories aloud to a friend or colleague and ask her to note the skills she heard. This is a great way to learn how you are perceived by others.

Transferable Lawyering Skills

This exercise focuses on two kinds of skills: **transferable** and **legal skills**. It will provide you with a sense of the degree to which you feel competent in your skills and the degree to which you enjoy utilizing various skills.

> INSTRUCTIONS: For each skill listed, rate yourself on the following scale.
>
> 4 = Very Confident in your ability
> 3 = Competent in your ability
> 2 = Cautious about your ability
> 1 = Can't Assess

To adjust for the **enjoyment level**, add the value of 1 if a high level of satisfaction or pleasure is associated with the performance of the listed skill; subtract the value of 1 if you dislike using the skill. If you neither like nor dislike the skill, no adjustment is necessary. Record your totals for the various skill cluster areas.

PART 1: Transferable Skills*

Written Communication (Total _____)

____ Correspondence (answering inquires, initiating letters, soliciting business)
____ Editing
____ Creative/Expository Writing
____ Writing (reports, memos, proposals)
____ Technical Writing
____ Translating (foreign language, signing)

*Part I of this exercise is adapted from material designed by Laura Share Kalin, Director of Career Services and Alice Alexander, Assistant Dean of Cooperative Legal Education at Northeastern University School of Law; Park II is adapted from materials designed by Professor Brook K. Baker, Northeastern University School of Law.

Verbal Communication (Total _____)

___ Teaching/Training
___ Public Speaking
___ Persuading/Promoting/Selling
___ Explaining
___ Articulating (quality of oral expression)
___ Connecting (being understood)
___ Social Chatting

Interpersonal (Total _____)

___ Listening
___ Advising/Counseling
___ Interviewing (obtaining information)
___ Handling Complaints
___ Confronting
___ Negotiating
___ Mediating
___ Group Facilitating
___ Getting Along With Others
___ Politicking
___ "Reading" others

Organizational (Total _____)

___ Anticipating/Estimating
___ Prioritizing
___ Coordinating/Arranging (events)
___ Compiling/Gathering (data)
___ Classifying/Ordering (information)
___ Programming
___ Planning/Scheduling
___ Record Keeping
___ Meeting Deadlines

Intellectual (Total _____)

___ Conceptualizing (new ideas)
___ Analyzing (events, data, people)
___ Theorizing (drawing generalizations)

___ Comprehending highly technical materials
___ Predicting/Forecasting (trends)
___ Experimenting
___ Remembering Information

Managerial (Total _____)

___ Supervising/Leading
___ Organizing/Coordinating
___ Motivating Others
___ Initiating
___ Risk Taking
___ Delegating
___ Exercising Good Judgment
___ Accepting Responsibility
___ Deciding

Problem-Solving (Total _____)

___ Examining
___ Reviewing
___ Assessing (the performance of others)
___ Evaluating (programs, services)
___ Appraising (values)
___ Applying Knowledge to Improve a Situation or Benefit Others
___ Trouble Shooting
___ Resolving Conflicts

Coping (Total _____)

___ Working Effectively and Calmly Under Pressure
___ Managing Time
___ Tolerating Delays/Waiting
___ Reserving
___ Accepting Criticism
___ Working Through Problems
___ Adjusting to Changes/Flexibility
___ Competing With Others

Numerical (Total _____)

___ Accounting/Bookkeeping
___ Allocating Resources
___ Managing Budgets
___ Using Computational Abilities
___ Estimating/Projecting (costs, income)
___ Developing Mathematical/Economic Models
___ Working With Precision
___ Financial Record Keeping
___ Inventorying
___ Using Statistical Abilities

Presenting (Total _____)

___ Exhibiting/Setting up
___ Displaying Ideas in Artistic Form
___ Dramatizing (ideas, social concerns)
___ Designing Exhibits
___ Making Layouts (media print, public displays)
___ Representing ("x" to the public)
___ Meeting the Public

Creativity (Total _____)

___ Inventing
___ Imagining
___ Designing
___ Applying Theory
___ Being an "Idea" person
___ Displaying
___ Constructing/Building
___ Assembling
___ Fixing

Playing (Total _____)

___ Music (singing, composing, playing instrument)
___ Dancing
___ Drawing/Painting/Sculpting
___ Competing at sports/games

___ Acting
___ Using Humor
___ Other "play": _____

PART 2 - Lawyering Skills

Legal Knowledge (Total _____)

___ Possess substantive knowledge of basic areas of law
___ Possess substantive knowledge of your particular area of expertise
___ Keep abreast of current developments in the law
___ Possess broad general knowledge of other areas of law in order to "red flag" issues and refer cases to others possessing expertise.

Legal Research (Total _____)

___ Perform research (case law and statutory) in a thorough, organized and competent manner
___ Know various secondary and primary research resources
___ Know how to use indexes
___ Know how to plan a research strategy
___ Familiar with computerized research resources
___ Know how to take systematic, useful research notes

Factual Research (Total _____)

___ Know how to plan fact investigations to obtain desired information
___ Know formal discovery devices and how to use them, including depositions, interrogatories and document requests
___ Know how to respond to formal discovery within ethical restraints to disclose required information

Legal Writing (Total _____)

___ Plan and organize writing by outline or otherwise so that it is coherent, logical and persuasive
___ Draft, redraft, and edit your writing critically
___ Produce well written, good quality legal documents
___ Use language clearly, precisely, and concisely

Legal Analysis (Total _____)

___ Understand how to analyze a case and analogize it to client facts
___ Understand how to analyze a statute or regulation and apply it to a client problem
___ Understand how to synthesize multiple cases and/or statutes
___ Understand how to select legal rules to apply to or distinguish from client or opponent facts
___ Combine legal analysis with common sense and problem-solving abilities
___ Develop creative and/or alternative approaches to problems
___ Develop appropriate strategy to serve client

Advocacy (Total _____)

___ Plan an effective trial strategy
___ Argue skillfully and effectively in court
___ Negotiate disputes skillfully and effectively
___ Prepare witnesses for examination
___ Examine witnesses using rules of evidence effectively
___ Develop ability to determine the credibility of witnesses, clients and testimony
___ Develop ability to determine the efficacy of opposing arguments
___ Practice appropriate courtroom demeanor and courtesy

Problem Solving (Total _____)

___ Negotiate transactional agreements
___ Help clients with strategic planning

___ Advise clients regarding compliance with applicable laws and regulations

Client Relations (Total _____)

___ Conduct sessions that leave the client informed and reassured
___ Understand client's goals
___ Provide realistic assessments
___ Nurture and develop new client base
___ Keep client apprised of progress/status of case
___ Prepare bills reflecting accurately accounted time

Substantive Legal Knowledge (Total _____)

___ Constitutional Law/Litigation
___ Federal courts
___ Commercial Law (U.C.C.)
___ Corporations
___ Corporate Finance
___ Entertainment Law
___ Environmental Law
___ Antitrust
___ Bankruptcy
___ Legal Accounting
___ Securities Regulations
___ Evidence
___ Criminal Advocacy/Procedure
___ Juvenile Law
___ Equitable Remedies
___ Land Use Planning
___ Administrative Law
___ Family Law
___ Estate Planning
___ Trusts and Estates
___ Welfare Law
___ Health Law
___ International Law
___ Comparative Law
___ Conflict of Law
___ Professional Responsibility
___ Labor Law
___ Collective Bargaining
___ Negotiation
___ Torts II
___ Intellectual Property
___ Immigration Law
___ Discrimination Law
___ Tax Law
___ Corporate Taxation
___ Legislation

EVALUATING ASSESSMENT INSTRUMENTS

Your law school Career Planning Center or a career counselor can assist you in identifying your motives, values, skills and goals by introducing you to the variety of "assessment" instruments available.

"Testing" has become a prominent feature of Career Planning because it can provide a wealth of information and a framework for highlighting your skills and accomplishments. All of these "tests" really are not tests—they are simply surveys of your values, interests, likes, dislikes and personal traits. There are no right or wrong answers, your answers are simply compared to other responses. For example:

Interest Inventories show how closely your interests match those of people who work successfully in various professions. The Strong Interest Inventory and the Self-Directed Search are two examples of Interest inventories.

Personality, Temperament & Values Questionnaires reveal similarities between how you approach various situations and the approaches other people say they would take. These tests can help you learn whether you are big picture oriented or detail oriented; whether you prefer to be part of a team or an independent player. The Myers Briggs Type Indicator is perhaps the best known example of these inventories.

Lawyers, who spend their careers trying to qualify everything, sometimes expect these inventories will lead to the perfect job. They won't. All that they can do is provide you with feedback about yourself which could change the way you conduct yourself in interviews. Before investing money on this process, consider going through the exercises in *What Color is Your Parachute* (Richard Bolles) or *If You Knew Who You Were You Could Be Who You Are* (Gerald M. Sturman, Ph.D.) Again, your law school's Career Planning Center can assist you in interrupting the results.

For more information about self-assessment testing, contact:

Center for the Application of Psychological Type (CAPT)
Phone: 1-800-777-CAPT

The Association for Psychological Type (APT)
Phone: 1-800-444-3500

Consulting Psychologist Press (CPP)
Phone: 1-800-6224-1765

When you can complete the following form, you will be ready to enter step two of your Business Plan.

I am seeking a position as a _____

in a setting such as_____
(Organization type)

in _____
(Geography)

utilizing my special knowledge in the areas of_____,

_____, _____, _____.

My skills in _____, _____, &_____

should be helpful in achieving my goal(s) of _____

_____

_____.

5

ANALYZING YOUR MARKET: CAREER EXPLORATION

Once you can articulate your strengths, skills, motives and goals, you need to find out who would be interested in the "product" you are selling.

Survey what is available in your area of interest in order to uncover what the market's needs are. Remember, do not be so narrowly focused that you can not see options outside of what you have been doing. Think about different ways to apply your skills. For example, if you are an intellectual property lawyer, consider computer companies, publishing companies, high tech businesses or entertainment enterprises. You may know enough about an industry to go into the business side. If you represent investment bankers, consider the financial services industry.

Real estate lawyers may want to present themselves as work out specialists. Consider how the topical issues of the day affect various industries and their legal implications. Also, be prepared to consider searching for opportunities in small, less visible firms and organizations or in other cities.

LIBRARY RESEARCH

As a lawyer, you already possess the well-developed research skills needed to gather information. Effective research will help you:

1. Identify people and organizations doing the type of work you want to do.
2. Understand how your skills can be used by those people and organizations.
3. Learn the "language" used in different job settings or alternative careers.
4. Design more thoughtful questions to ask of your contacts.
5. Bring a sense of structure and coherence to a chaotic job market.

Without research, you are placing your job search in the hands of chance. You would never think of risking a client's future to chance by representing him in front of an adversary without conducting proper research first. Likewise you should never represent yourself to potential employers without conducting proper research first.

Even though there will be a lot of growth opportunities with **small law firms** in the nineties, identifying them will continue to present unique challenges for job seekers. Many small firms do not list in Martindale-Hubbell or produce corporate brochures or other marketing pieces, making research difficult. In addition to using Lexis/Nexis or Westlaw to run searches by individual attorney names, consider using more creative approaches. For example, contact your law school's Alumni Office for a copy of the Alumni Directory. Successful sole practitioners and small organizations know that keeping in touch with their schools is good for business. Consider joining local bar associations as another way to meet people and see "who knows who." Also, don't forget to use the phone book! This will help you add local practitioners to your contact list.

A visit to the public library can uncover a wealth of information. Most libraries are stocked with company directories and other reference books to help you learn about industries and develop target lists of organizations. You can also uncover information regarding salaries, work hours, the ability to develop clients and levels of practice in different localities. Look for:

MAJOR PUBLICATIONS

Encyclopedia of Associations
Gale Research, Inc.
Provides summary information on nearly 25,000 associations, including size, offices, publications, and services.

Encyclopedia of Business Information
Gale Research, Inc.
Includes analyses of 300+ service industries, i.e. stats, geographic analysis, occupations employed, leading companies, and related information.

Occupational Outlook Handbook
U.S. Department of Labor
Describes more than 250 occupations, provides salary ranges and projects hiring demand to the year 2000.)

United States Industrial Outlook
U.S. Department of Labor
Provides general information about various industries; discusses trends and forecasts for 35 industries.

Legal Connection
Data Financial Press
Lists 5000 publicly held companies and the 2000 firms that are linked to them.

David White and Associates Annual Attorney Salary Survey
David J. White & Associates, Inc.
Lists salaries for lawyers by firm size and geographic location.

National Business Employment Weekly
DOW Jones and Company, Inc.
This weekly newspaper publishes *"Cost of Living Statistics"* quarterly, comparing numbers for over 100 U.S. cities along with

an equation to help you compare salary offers. *"Relocation Guidance"* profiles cities, providing demographic data, cost-of-living and tax indexes, telephone numbers for major realtors, executive recruiters, employment agencies and employers. Includes information articles and vacancy announcements.

GOVERNMENT/PUBLIC INTEREST DIRECTORIES

Register of U.S. Department of Justice and the Federal Courts
U.S. Government Printing Office
Provides names, offices and appointment dates for departments within the Department of Justice and the Federal Courts.

Congressional Quarterly's Federal Regulatory Directory
Congressional Quarterly, Inc.
Profiles the thirteen largest regulatory agencies; includes discussions of the agency's powers and responsibilities, biographies of agency commissioners or board members and organizational charts for each agency. Also profiled are 100 important regulatory agencies both independent and within the executive department. These profiles include responsibilities, organizational information, telephone contact lists, regional offices—addresses and contacts and coverage of any on-line computer access.

Federal Law—Related Careers
Federal Reports, Inc.
Lists law related careers in the federal government which include descriptions of duties and responsibilities, the number of current positions, federal grade levels, average annual salary, federal agencies employing people in that field and how to inquire about direct hire opportunities.

Federal Careers for Attorneys, Inc.
Federal Reports
Contains detailed descriptions of the legal work and application requirements of over 300 federal legal offices and cites the location of over 1,400 regional/field offices.

United States Lawyers Reference Directory (six volumes)
Legal Directories Publishing Company
Each volume lists specific state governments, its departments, addresses, executive officers, phone numbers, tax departments, court sections, bar sections and city county lists with city officials, addresses and telephone numbers. Also included are judges, their clerks, court recorders, county attorneys, county auditors, numbers and addresses for county and city jails and sheriffs departments.

Congressional Directory
U.S. Government Printing Office, Washington, DC
Lists members of both the House and the Senate with brief biographical sketches of members, district descriptions, and also committee assignments. Also includes a list of executive departments, the main officers, and addresses and phone numbers of department offices. Another section includes information on governmental agencies, and the Judiciary. Includes maps of Congressional districts along with statistical information on these districts.

New York State Directory
Walker's Western Research Inc.
Provides direct informational access to officials in the executive, legislative and judicial branches of the New York State Government. Also included in this directory are Federal departments, agencies and members of Congress who play a role in defining State programs and policies. Any individuals in the private sector who may influence these areas are also included when the information is available and applicable. The key contacts to the Governor, Lieutenant Governor, members of the New York State Legislature and the Judicial branch are also included with addresses and phone numbers. The 25 biggest policy areas are outlined along with information identifying contact agencies and state legislators who are involved in formulating and implementing government regulation in these areas.

Congressional Quarterly's: Washington Information Directory
Congressional Quarterly, Inc.
Dealing only with the Washington D.C. area, the directory includes information on the federal government, Congress or the private, nonprofit sector. Each entry includes the name, address

and telephone number of the organization, the name and title of the director and a brief description of the work performed by the organization. The directory is divided into three categories: agencies, Congress and non-governmental organizations.

Congressional Yellow Book
Leadership Directories Inc.
Provides useful telephone numbers for both the House and the Senate, scheduling information, where to get records, and the current status of bills. Divided into seven sections. **Section 1** deals with State Delegates. This section begins with each state listed alphabetically and senators listed in order of seniority. The senators are listed by their political party, the state which they represent, their (re-election) year, office locations, telephone and fax numbers, e-mail addresses, professions prior to election and the Committees on which they serve. Also listed is brief information on the senator's staff. **Section 2** contains similar information on Representatives and their Staffs. **Sections 3, 4 and 5** covers the Senate, the House of Representatives and Joint Committees. Each section lists all committees, members by seniority, telephone numbers and locations of subcommittees and individual staff. **Section 6** deals with the Senate and the House leadership and Party related organizations; lists members and additional information on the goal of the specific organization. **Section 7** includes Congressional Support Agencies such as Budget Offices, General Accounting Office, Printing Offices and the Library of Congress. The Senior personnel in these support agencies are listed along with addresses and telephone numbers.

Municipal Yellow Book
Leadership Directories, Inc.
Provides information on cities and counties. The cities are listed with main addresses, telephone numbers, mayor, city council members and their staffs. Specifies its county seat name and personnel listings of officers for each city. The same information is included in the county listings. Lists nation's top authorities along with their addresses and phone numbers.

Federal Yellow Book
Leadership Directories, Inc.
Designed to allow the user easy access to the top people in the

Executive Branch of the Federal Government. Divided into the four following sections: 1) Executive office of the President/VP, 2) The Fourteen Executive Departments, 3) Independent Agencies and 4) Indexes. Each section lists the names, addresses and telephone numbers of the key people in the executive branch of the government. Includes additional information on whether they are a presidential appointee or a member of the Senior Executive Service system (those in this system are ranked just below presidential appointees) along with frequently used phone numbers.

Directory of the National Support Centers
National Clearinghouse for Legal Services
Profiles sixteen Support Centers funded by Legal Services that provide a variety of specialized services that promote quality representation of the poor on issues of substantial complexity. Each Center's service is described in detail. Provides main office address, telephone and fax numbers. Each Center's description is broken down into the following six areas: Project Description, Available Resources, Typical Requests for Assistance, Service Request Policy, Staff, and Board of Directors.

Public Interest Law Groups: Institutional Profiles
Greenwood Press
Provides detailed profiles of Public Interest groups that are active in the American Legal system. Includes addresses, a brief history and general overview of the law and cases that are undertaken by the individual groups.

LAW FIRMS AND LAWYER DIRECTORIES

Martindale-Hubbell
Reed Publishing
Consists of Sixteen U.S. volumes, separated into three main sections: Practice Profiles, Professional Biographies and Services, and Consultants. One volume containing listings for Corporate Law Departments and Law Schools. Two Alphabetical Index Volumes. Two Areas of Practice Index Volumes. Three International Law Directory Volumes containing listings for lawyers

and firms in over 130 countries and Three digest volumes.

NALP Directory of Legal Employers
National Association for Law Placement
Includes statistical information such as areas of practice, size of organization, number of partners and associates, including ethnic and gender breakdowns, starting salaries and billable hours on more than 1100 employers nationwide.

Law Firms: Yellow Book—Winter 1995
Leadership Directories Inc.
Published semi-annually, The Law Firm Yellow Book, covers 714 law firms with specific emphasis on their organizational and business structure. It focuses specifically on attorney and administrative personnel responsible for management and decision making policies. The law firms are listed alphabetically by name with addresses and communication information. General Information on each firm includes the year the firm was founded, the number of attorneys practicing, specific networks that the firm belongs to plus a brief practice description of the major practice area departments. There is a management section that lists information on the members of the firms major governing committees. The Administration section contains lists of chief administrators of the firms. The U.S. offices of the law firms are listed with their top management and administrative personnel, these are listed alphabetically by state and then by city. The listing also includes any subsidiaries or affiliates.

Of Counsel 700
Aspen Hall Law & Business
An annual survey of the Nation's 700 largest law firms. Each law firm's description includes growth patterns, practice areas, partner and associate demographics, paralegals, billing rates, revenues, branch offices and firm leaders.

Who's Who in American Law
Marquis Who's Who
Provides biographical information on approximately 30,000 lawyers and law related professionals. Examples of information included are individual's education, career history, awards, memberships and areas of expertise or interest.

The American Bar: Reference Handbook
Forster-Long, Inc.
This reference directory is divided into two sections: 1) an Individual Attorney Index and 2) Firm Name and Location Index. Each index is divided alphabetically by state and then by firm name. Information includes firm names, addresses, telephone numbers, members and location.

The Lawyer's Almanac
Aspen Hall Law & Business
Includes a detailed list of the nation's 500 largest law firms; which firms are growing; the firm's major practice areas and staff data. There is a complete text of mandatory continuing legal education requirements for the 39 state jurisdictions that have them. There is also an expanded list of bankruptcy courts, judges and court personnel. The Almanac is divided into five sections which are as follows: 1) The Legal Profession—500 of the largest law firms plus 50 of the largest corporate legal departments, billing rates (city by city), associate salaries, contact information, principal officers and annual meeting dates for all state bar associations; 2) The Judiciary—location of all federal courts; names of all federal judges and of chief justices, their terms and qualifications, specific data on the selection process, survey of state court salaries and litigation statistics for federal courts; 3) Government Departments and Agencies—listed are the names, addresses and phone numbers of the U.S. Attorney, State Attorney General, banking authority, securities commissioners, mental health program directors and how to locate birth, death, marriage and divorce records; 4) Statutory Summaries and Checklists—state laws governing handguns, motorist liability and chemical testing; and 5) Commonly Used Abbreviations.

Law and Legal Information Directory, Volumes I & II
Gale Research Inc.
Describes organizations, services, programs about the legal field and also directs reader to current facts and details in the legal field. The following are new areas that have been added to this edition: State Lawyer Disciplinary Agencies, Environmental Protection Offices, Banking Authorities, Food and Drug Agency Offices, Departments of Public Health and Housing, Commissioners of Insurance, OSHA, Education Department, Public Utility Com-

missions and Consumer Protection Offices; their addresses, telephone numbers and contact people are included. The Directory is divided into 40 sections which usually contain the name of the organization, phone number, addresses, officials and titles, any activities, publications and usually a brief description about the organization.

Directory of Environmental Attorneys
Aspen Hall Law & Business
Includes information on more than 9200 attorneys and nearly 4500 law firms, companies and regulatory agencies. Arranged geographically and provides addresses, number of attorneys who practice in this area and the number of offices maintained by the organizations as well as individual attorney biographies. It also arranges information by the following indexes: Law School Alumni, Area of Concentration, Regulatory Agency Experience, Attorneys, and Firm/Organization.

Directory of Entertainment and Sports Attorneys
Aspen Hall Law & Business
Includes information on more than 3200 attorneys and nearly 2500 organizations. This book is arranged geographically and provides addresses, number of attorneys who practice in this area and the number of offices maintained by the organizations as well as individual attorney biographies. It also arranges information by the following indexes: Law School Alumni, Area of Concentration, Foreign Languages, Types of Clients, Attorneys, and Firm/Organization.

Directory of Intellectual Property Attorneys
Aspen Hall Law & Business
Arranged geographically, this directory provides addresses, number of attorneys who practice in this area and the number of offices maintained by the organizations as well as individual attorney biographies. It also arranges information by the following indexes: Law School Alumni, Special Knowledges, Foreign Languages, Attorneys and Patent Agents, and Firm/Organization.

Directory of Litigation Attorneys
Aspen Hall Law & Business
Contains information on over 39,000 attorneys and 14,000 law

firms. Each volume in this two volume set is divided into five sections: Attorney Biographies, Firm Descriptions, Area of Concentration, Attorney Index, and Firm Index.

Directory of Bankruptcy Attorneys
Thomas Redding & Associates
Arranged by State, each section begins with a map highlighting the Bankruptcy Clerks' office location and the other cities where the court meets. The biographies of the attorneys are listed under the city in which that attorney most frequently appears. Individual attorney and firm indexes are provided.

Desk Reference
The Association of Trial Lawyers of America
Lists members of the association, their addresses and phone numbers. It also has a comprehensive list of committees, their purpose, members of the committee with addresses and phone numbers.

The Medical Malpractice Defense and Health Care Counsel Directory
Professional Reports Corporation
This is a nationwide selection of law firms and attorneys with important background information included. Addresses and phone numbers as well as hourly rates and a list of representative clients are also included.

Lawyer's Register International by Specialties and Fields of Law
Lawyer's Register Publishing Co.
This registry is a list of lawyers and law firms both across the country and internationally who represent themselves as certified or designated practitioners who specialize or concentrate their practices in one or more specified fields of law. The fields of specialty are listed alphabetically.

National Directory of Criminal Lawyers
Gold Publishers
This directory was developed to be a source for evaluating the ability and commitment of criminal lawyers throughout the nation. It is divided into two categories. Lawyers were placed in Category I if they fulfilled the following criteria: 1) had been in practice a

minimum of 10 years; 2) have developed an outstanding reputation and significant practice; 3) are able and willing to deliver competent legal representation; and 4) other lawyers polled would retain them if in need of a criminal defense attorney. Those placed in Category II have not necessarily developed a substantial practice or reputation, but because of outstanding ability and background, lawyers polled would retain them if in need of a criminal lawyer.

The American Bar: Lawyers of the World
Forster-Long, Inc.

This set contains two volumes which include an Individual Attorney Index and Firm Name and Location Index and a Canadian and International Patent and Trademark Agents. Also included is a listing of American Law Schools. Each firm has a description of the nature of the practice, including individual biographies of firm members and representative clients. There is a firm history with the range of hourly rates for the firm. Any of the cities or towns named are followed by the population figures and county names.

CORPORATE DIRECTORIES

Directory of Corporate Counsel
Prentice Hall Law and Business

Provides information on more than 7000 corporations and non-profit organizations plus thousands of subsidiaries, divisions and affiliates and over 33,000 attorneys. Companies are listed alphabetically by name, with attorney biographies following each listing. Indexes are provided by Attorneys, Geography, Corporation/Organization, Subject Index to Non-Profit Organizations and Law School Alumni.

Yearbook of International Organizations (three volumes)
K.G. Swear

The purpose of this yearbook is to try to give informational access to all international organizations. The organizations are listed alphabetically, with addresses, what year they were founded, the business structure, activities, publications, a list of members, languages that are spoken, how the organization is financed and any events that the organization sponsors.

Standard & Poor's Register of Corporations, Directories and Executives (three volumes)
McGraw-Hill Inc.
Alphabetical listing of over 55,000 corporations which includes addresses, telephone numbers plus the names, titles and functions of approximately 500,000 officers and directors. Other information also included is the name of the company's accounting firm, primary bank, law firm and the stock exchange on which the company is traded, the annual sales, the number of employees, a list of subsidiaries and affiliations along with a brief description of the company's products. The Individual listings of directors and executives are alphabetically organized to include over 70,000 individuals servings as officers, directors, trustees, and partners. Each listing includes the title, address and phone numbers along with brief biographical information.

JUDICIAL DIRECTORIES

The National Directory of Courts of Law
Informational Resources Press
Lists various court systems and the means to communicate with each court. The courts are listed in the reverse order of route of appeal and/or descending order of jurisdiction. The directory is broken down into the following four parts: Federal Courts; State Courts and the District of Columbia; Courts of Territories; and Courts of Native American Tribes.

Judicial Staff Directory
Congressional Staff Directory, Ltd.
This directory is divided into seven major sections: **1) Federal Courts**: The courts are arranged by the circuits of the U.S. Court of Appeals. Includes the names of the cities in which the court sits, the states within the courts jurisdiction and the addresses for the court. It also lists the members of the court in seniority order, plus the Court Staff is listed for each judge. **2) Department of Justice**: Includes the executives and officers of the Department in hierarchical order with addresses and numbers. **3) Counties and Cities and their Circuits and Districts**: Listed alphabetically by states all U.S. counties with their 1990 census counts and the circuits and districts in which they are located. **4) Maps of Court Jurisdiction. 5) Index of Judges**: Each judge is listed alpha-

betically; by year of appointment and by appointing President. **6) Biographies of Judges & Staff**: The biographies of federal judges arranged alphabetically. **7) Index of Individuals**: Lists all the individuals named in the book alphabetically with page references.

The American Bench: Judges of the Nation
Forster-Long, Inc.
This resource is divided into two sections: 1) Alphabetical Name Index—lists the names of judges, their titles, the courts the judges sit on and the states they serve. 2) The Structure of the Court Systems—Court outlines that include the judicial structure of each state listed alphabetically. This section also includes biographical data on each judge listed alphabetically under the state in which they serve.

BNA's Directory of State & Federal Courts, Judges and Clerks
The Bureau of National Affairs, Inc.
This directory has listings for over 2,000 state courts and 100 federal courts. Court structures and the path of appeals are depicted by charts. Each court entry contains the name of the court, clerks, judges and geographic jurisdiction. The clerk section includes information on names, addresses and fax numbers. Judges are listed alphabetically, by seniority, court division or title. The directory also contains lists of Federal and State level administrators.

The Directory of Minority Judges in the United States
American Bar Association
This directory is broken down into the following four sections African American, Asian/Pacific Islander, Hispanic and Native American. Each section is then alphabetical by state, lists the total number of minority judges by state, gives the address and telephone number of each judge.

This list is by no means exhaustive, but it should be enough to get you started.

IDENTIFYING CONTACTS

The primary goal in conducting library research is to identify people to contact and develop thoughtful questions to ask them. Library research alone is not sufficient so do not spend an excessive amount of time simply reading and taking notes. Your time can be better spent gathering information by talking to people. Unlike books, people will have more current, detailed and accurate information about what is happening in the field.

Contacts are your single most valuable resource in the job search. It is extremely important to utilize these relationships as a primary outreach technique to broaden your field of vision in preparation for making a good career decision.

Networking means simply meeting in person with professional and personal contacts (even if you have been out of touch for a long time) and asking for ideas and advice on the ways your talents could be used by organizations. Networking rests on the basic principle that businesses, jobs and careers are built on personal relationships. Law school classmates and professors, college friends and family members, former employers, colleagues and opponents, and bar association leaders may be able to assist you.

The true purpose of networking is to get information, advice and referrals; it occurs naturally in all areas of life. For example, when moving into a new neighborhood, you probably would not hesitate to ask your new neighbors for recommendations about dry cleaners, grocery stores, dentists, etc. Or when planning a vacation you would not think twice about asking friends or family to recommend hotels and restaurants. In business it is common to ask colleagues to suggest accountants, bankers or computer systems. But for some reason, we hesitate to ask people we know about job opportunities.

The advertised job market represents only about 25% of actual openings. This market tends to represent positions at the extreme ends of the job spectrum—low paid unskilled or high-paid highly skilled jobs. Worst of all, many of these advertised jobs are actually filled prior to being advertised. **Given that more than 75% of job changes result from networking, this is the most important job search activity.** Word of mouth communication is still the most practical route of job search information. Furthermore, effective networking can provide job seekers with a sense of control because it provides a focus and structure for receiving information during a very stressful period.

Countless books and articles have been written outlining networking techniques and gimmicks to coach readers. But you can not be effective with empty techniques and gimmicks. **Think through your strategy first.** You need to have a clear objective about what you are trying to accomplish before you visit anyone! There should be no hidden agenda.

At this point in your search you should simply be looking for information about where the jobs are.

It is important to understand what you can reasonably expect from relationships and what is outside those bounds. It is **not** reasonable to expect **a job** will be handed to you! When networking to uncover job opportunities, it is reasonable to expect:

Moral Support
Assistance in formulating plans
To receive feedback about resumes, cover letters and approach
Testing of ideas and theories
Education about the world of works
Referrals to others who can help you
Suggestions

Clearly, networking MATTERS!

Most people do not know of many current job openings. If the first and only question posed to your contacts is "Do you know of any openings?" you will more often than not receive a **no** and an opportunity may be lost. By asking "What do you do and what alternatives are out there?" you will uncover information which will eventually generate job leads and preserve your relationships.

It is important not to concentrate your efforts on only those with influential positions and the power to hire you. Remember, networking should only be used as a communication process to acquire information, **not** as a manipulation used to acquire power and influence over employers. If you are playing the "advice and information game" when you really believe networking is nothing more than the back door route to a new position, you are being insincere, misleading and you will not be effective. Focus on people who are close to your level of experience—it is less uncomfortable networking with fellow professionals than with potential employers.

While appearing to be organized and coherent, the job market really is disorganized and chaotic. Your task is to organize the chaos around your skills and interests. Having identified a market need, you now must be able to outline and explain how you think you can fill the need. By talking to people—family, friends, clients, opposing counsel, people you meet on airplanes—you can learn new information and reassess your options. Job searches are so much easier when you have a defined target employment setting or a specific way you'd like to use your skills. Seek advice from experts and adapt ideas to your needs. Do what is right for you in the context of your particular circumstances.

OVERCOMING THE FEAR OF BEING LABELED A "USER"

Many people are hesitant about "using" people or asking for help. However, networking should be viewed as a communication process—exchanging and receiving advice and referrals about jobs. Many people these days consider it foolish **not** to use contacts, and those in a position to help you might even be insulted that they were not asked for assistance. People **like** to help others. It makes them feel good, powerful and important. By establishing a specific and relevant basis for a meeting—asking for ideas, opinions, a reaction to your own thoughts—there is no reason for you to be turned down. Ask for something specific, something doable.

Consider the following sample approaches to potential contacts:

To a Geographic contact: "You have lived in this city for so long and know almost everyone..."

To a socially active friend: "You have so many friends, you probably hear about things before anyone..."

To someone who works in your field: "You've been working in the same type of job I am looking for, I am sure you have some idea how my skills might be viewed..."

To a professor: "You know better than anyone what kinds of jobs are open in this field..."

To anyone you admire: "You always seem to have good ideas..."

To someone you have helped: "We have helped each other in the past, so I am hoping you can help me now..."

Since much of professional life operates on the "favor system," establish a reputation for being helpful. Pass along useful information or introduce contacts to people you have met along the way that could be helpful to them. Look for ways to build bridges. People will remember your thoughtfulness and will be likely to return the favor. Busy professionals understand the system and they know that with just a little time and some guidance from **you** they can evaluate you for their own needs or those of their colleagues while still satisfying your request for information. Both you and the other person receive something. Therefore, don't feel guilty about approaching busy people for help; they will enjoy it and you will benefit by it. If you are doubtful, consider whether you would be willing to share your knowledge or give names to friends or business associates in order to be helpful.

You should be concerned with the process of building and using networks as a permanent aspect of your career, not just a technique you use for finding jobs and advancing your career. Keep in touch with people you meet. Drop them a note occasionally or send them an article you saw that made you think of them. When you do land a job, let your contacts know. Do not wait until you "need" something from them. **It is important to develop, use and nurture personal relationships on a daily basis throughout your career.**

YOU'RE READY TO NETWORK

When you can respond affirmatively to **all** of these statements, you are ready to network!

___ I have prepared a list of potential contacts.

___ I have thought through my strategy and can articulate a clear objective for meeting with specific contacts.

___ I have thoroughly researched organizations I am interested in exploring.

___ I can articulate my strengths, skills, motives, and goals.

___ I am positive and upbeat and fully expect the meeting to be successful.

___ I present myself in a professional manner, dressing in a way that projects a positive image.

6

WORKING A ROOM: JOB PROSPECTING

Consider using professional associations like the American Bar Association and local bar organizations as a source of networking. And, be creative. For example, if you have identified a firm or organization in which you have an interest, find out what social events they host and get yourself invited. Or find out what pro bono activities they are involved in and volunteer yourself. Chances are if the partner or general counsel are present, associates and other members of the organization will be too. Your goal should be to make friends first; you can probe for information and openings later. The important thing is to attend events and work the room.

"Working a room" is the ability to circulate comfortably and graciously through a gathering of people. People who are most successful at it are those who genuinely like people. There is nothing calculated or manipulative about it because the process is based on mutual interests. Remind yourself what has brought this particular group of people together and why it is important for you to be there.

Anxiety often allows people to talk themselves out of attending a worthwhile event. The fear of walking alone into a room filled with strangers is pervasive, cutting across boundaries of age, sex, race, socioeconomic level, professional and personal experience. But, do whatever it takes to silence those discouraging voices in your head and motivate yourself to **go**! Bring a friend; promise yourself a treat; buy a new outfit appropriate to the occasion that inspires confidence. Reassure yourself that once you are there, you will be fine. And, in the worst case scenario, if you **are** truly as miserable as those little voices told you you would be, you can always leave.

FIVE IMPEDIMENTS TO WORKING A ROOM

In order to successfully work a room you will have to overcome 5 major obstacles and be prepared to challenge some deeply ingrained societal beliefs you always considered to be non-negotiable.

1. **An aggressive approach to socializing is impolite**.

   We have grown up believing that it is tacky to use people for personal gain. Being polite means being unobtrusive, not asking direct questions, not talking about our personal lives and drawing as little attention to ourselves as possible. But, by freely acknowledging that attending an event is good for you because it will provide you with the opportunity to develop business, or to have a more active social life, or because it makes you feel good to support a cause or make new friends, or because it provides you with access to potential employers, you will eliminate the feeling of "dishonesty" and "tackiness" and be able to enjoy the event.

2. **One should not talk to strangers**.

   Ever since we were children our parents instilled a fear in us about talking to people we did not know. One way to overcome this obstacle would be to consider what it is we have in common with others at the event. Are they all fellow attorneys or alumni or parents or church members or supporters of a political candidate, etc.? Determining the common bond makes it easier to approach people because then they are no longer "strangers." You can then begin a conversation based on the common bond.

3. One needs to be properly introduced.

Because it is not always feasible to be introduced by a mutual acquaintance you may need to "properly introduce" yourself. Design an 10-15 second introduction that is clear, interesting and well-delivered. Your goal should be not only to tell people who you are but also to **give people a pleasant experience of you**. Naturally, what you say will depend on the nature of the event. For example:

- At an ABA convention: "Hello, my name is Lisa Green. I am an intellectual property attorney from NYC."
- At a wedding: "Hello, my name is Lisa Green. I am a former college roommate of the bride."

Remember, the most important person you can introduce yourself to is the host. It is that person's job to make sure everyone is having a good time and the host will help you to meet other people in the room.

4. Fear of rejection.

This obstacle is more imagined than real. Very few people will be openly hostile or rude, if for no other reason than that it is bad business. To help overcome this fear, try adapting a "host mentality." Hosts are concerned with the comfort of others and actively contribute to that comfort. By focusing on making others feel welcomed and included, you will become more comfortable. If you **are** met with rudeness, do not take it personally. There may be a hundred reasons why that person is not receptive. Simply move on.

5. Discomfort with small talk.

If you read a newspaper, you are ready for small talk! Also, reading special interest publications can give you a quick overview of what is happening in any business region. Check the directory called ***Bacon's Publicity Checker*** which lists over 17,000 magazines, journals and newsletters indexed by categories that cover everything.

ENTERING THE ROOM

When you arrive at the event, quickly scan the room. Try and get a sense of the crowd. Note where the bar and food are located. See if anyone you know is already there. If so, go say hello. That is the quickest entree to meeting other people. If you do not recognize any familiar faces, try positioning yourself somewhere between the entry and the buffet table. This will enable a friend or colleague (also seeking the quickest entree to the group) to see you; it will also ensure that you will always be surrounded by people.

If nametags are available, they should be worn on your right hand side, making it easy to scan as you shake hands. "As your hand goes out, your name goes forward." Remember to write legibly (and largely) including all pertinent information that seems appropriate to the occasion.

OPENING LINES

Adopting your host mentality, approach someone who is standing alone and say: "I don't believe we have met. My name is..."(use your 10-15 second introduction).

To get a conversation started you may want to:

- Share an observation about the situation. Comment on the facility, food, organization, traffic, parking dilemma, etc. Remember, the comment ought to be positive and upbeat. Look for those bridges that have led the two of you to be in the same room.

- Ask an open-ended question. (**Examples**: "How long have you been a member of this organization?" "How do you fit into this picture?" "How do you know the bride or groom?") Be careful not to fire off too many questions; you want to engage people in a conversation—not make them feel like they are being interrogated.

- Reveal something about yourself. Disclosing something about yourself helps to establish vulnerability and approachability. (**Example**: "I had such a hard time finding this place and I only work 5 blocks away!") Volunteering information about yourself will make the other person feel safe about doing the same. Be careful not to reveal anything too personal which may burden the listener. (**Example**: "My wife just told me she wants a divorce.")

EXIT LINES

The objective of attending an event is to meet a number of people, so it is important to circulate. Your goal should be to spend about 8 to 10 minutes with each person. This can be accomplished either by "lapping" the room or by strategically positioning yourself in the flow of traffic.

Do not monopolize any one person's time, and do not allow your time to be monopolized by any one person. If someone has latched on to you, choose whether or not you want to make it your responsibility to take care of him/her throughout the night thereby missing other opportunities present in the room. To make an exit, offer a connecting gesture like a handshake or a pat on the arm or shoulder and simply say:

- "I am sure there are other people you need to talk to. I do not want to monopolize your time. It has been interesting speaking with you."
- "Excuse me, it was nice meeting you."
- "Excuse me, there is someone I need to say hello to." (Make sure you move to another part of the room.)

To join the next group, simply say:

- "Excuse me for interrupting, but I wanted to say hello."

Another option would be to position yourself close to a group already engaged in conversation. Avoid groups which appear to be engaged in private, intimate conversations. Give facial feedback to comments. When you feel included (usually after you have established eye contact with someone in the group), feel free to join the conversation.

Remember to be open to others who may want to join a group you are already a part of. If you are doing the introductions, remember to "introduce up." Bluntly put, that means introduce the person with the lesser title to the person with the higher title (associate to the partner, partner to judge, etc.)

Business cards are a must, whether you are employed or not, as you may want to facilitate the exchange of information with people you meet. Place your business cards in an easy to reach place. You may want to invest in an attractive card carrying case. Once you have established rapport and decided you are interested in exchanging cards, offer yours first. People will surely return in kind.

Remember, simply collecting business cards is not effective: being a participant is! Demonstrate your capabilities by becoming involved. That gives prospective employers the opportunity to witness your abilities first hand.

Do not rush to network at every occasion. Feel out the situation and use your judgment. If all you talk about is needing a job, people will run when they see you. **Your goal should be for people to have a pleasant, positive experience of you.** You do not need to "close the deal" at this event; you simply need to create an opening to use at a later point in time.

Follow-up is the key. Write a letter within one week of the event, reminding your contact where you met and about the conversation you had regarding a particular subject. Restate your interest in the subject and ask for what you need—15 minutes of her time for **advice** and **information**.

Finally, remember that you are completely responsible for what you bring into a room and for what you project onto other people. Dress like the confident professional that you are. Be positive and upbeat. Project a proud, confident image. If you look and act like a loser, that is how people will respond to you.

7

STRATEGIES FOR APPROACHING CONTACTS

Whether you have identified your contacts through library research or attending events, it is important to use a well thought-out process when approaching your contacts for assistance. An approach letter, followed by a phone call, informational interview and thank-you note is most effective. Write a letter then call to ask for 15 minutes of their time for **advice**. Do not put pressure on the individual to find you a job or to interview you. That may be a long term result, but at this juncture, an informative conversation should be your objective.

LETTER OF INTRODUCTION
(Sample)

Your Name
Street Address
City, State, Zip
Date

Contact Name
Title
Organization
Street Address
City, State, Zip Code

Dear:

Bob Smith suggested that I contact you about my interest in career opportunities in environmental law (the legal community in New Jersey, etc.) I am a graduate of XYZ Law School with 4 years experience in...

(Your next paragraph should tell something about your background. Include your prior work experience, current situation, skills, interests, academic history, connection to the geographic region, etc.)

As I venture into the job market, I hope to benefit from the experience and knowledge of others in the field (in New Jersey) who might advise me on opportunities for someone with my qualifications. I would appreciate the opportunity to meet with you for 15 minutes for your guidance. I will call your office next week to see if we can schedule a meeting.

I look forward to discussing my plans with you. Thank you for your consideration.

Sincerely,

Your Name

LETTER OF REINTRODUCTION
(Sample)

Your Name
Street Address
City, State, Zip
Date

Contact Name
Title
Organization
Street Address
City, State zip code

Dear:

It was a pleasure meeting you last week at _____. (Remind your contact where you met and the nature of your conversation. Restate your interest in the topic.)

(Your next paragraph should tell something about your background. Include your prior work experience, current situation, skills, interests, academic history, connection to the geographic region, etc.)

I would appreciate the opportunity to further discuss my job search strategies with you in order to benefit from your expertise. I will call your office next week to see if we can schedule a 15 minute meeting.

Enjoy the opera next week. (Close with some reference to your prior conversation.)

Thank you again for your help.

Sincerely,

Your Name

Do **not** include your resume with the letter. The receiver may assume you are applying for a job and may not bother to read the letter thereby missing your request. Simply supply any relevant information contained in your resume in paragraph two of the letter.

TELEPHONE SKILLS

Nothing is more effective than a well-written cover letter followed promptly (5 - 7 days later) by a telephone call. Most job seekers never even try to call decision-makers and even those who do, do not do so often enough. The telephone is the most underutilized tool available to the job seeker. With it, assertive candidates can reduce uncertainty and waiting time. It is your responsibility as the job seeker to make the telephone call and schedule a meeting!

Prepare a script so you can clearly and succinctly introduce yourself and articulate your needs. Your ability to present yourself and explain what you hope to gain from meeting with your contact will determine his response to you. Why have you chosen this particular firm and more importantly, this particular person to contact over all of the other possibilities? What specifically do you want to find out? These types of questions will help you to clarify your objectives in networking before you call or write contacts and will increase your chances of piquing their interest in meeting you. You must be prepared to say more than "I have just lost my job and I was wondering if you know of any openings." Consider instead:

> "Hello, Mr./Ms._____. This is Mary Brown, I am calling at the suggestion of Bob Smith. I sent you a letter last week explaining...(restate the first paragraph of your letter) and I was wondering if you might have 15 minutes next Tuesday or Thursday to meet with me?"

Remember, you do not want to exert pressure on this person to find you a job. You only want to explain the purpose of the meeting and articulate how you believe your contact can be helpful. The objective is to unearth information about them and their job experience.

Choose a private comfortable setting for making calls. Besides your script, keep a pen, pad and copy of your resume and letter at hand. Being prepared will help to ameliorate an attack of phone fright and will prevent you from omitting important information. Your script should include:

- who you are calling (address the person by name)
- who referred you
- why you are calling (to determine the status of your letter)
- how you believe the person could be helpful

As the example suggests, consider giving the listener a choice between something and something, not a choice between something and nothing. For example: "I was wondering if we might meet Tuesday afternoon or Thursday morning," is more effective than "I was wondering if we might meet next week." Even if both times are not convenient, offering a choice avoids complete rejection and steers the interviewer into discussing timing. Remember to confirm time and exact address, including floor and room number.

If the person seems hesitant to grant your request to meet, clearly state that you are not looking for a job with them and that you are only looking for advice and information. If you are still met with resistance, try to conduct the informational interview over the phone. If even that feels uncomfortable, politely bring the conversation to a close and than write a nice thank you letter, again stating your intended purpose. Mention your disappointment in not being able to learn from the person's experience and ask to be remembered for future reference. Enclose your resume with this letter.

STUMBLING BLOCKS: VOICE MAIL AND SECRETARIES

Perhaps the greatest challenge when using the telephone is reaching your target. The advent of phone mail has frustrated many job seekers. Be prepared to leave a detailed message of why you are calling and state a time when you will call back to alert your contact. **Do not simply leave a name and a phone number and expect a person to return your call.**

Reaching a receptionist or secretary can provide a unique set of problems. Keep in mind that it is part of their job to screen phone calls. Secretaries are trained to keep the unwanted world away from a busy boss.

Try to take control of the conversation from the beginning, following your script. Sound confident. If requested to give a reason for the call, offer, "She is expecting my call. We have corresponded," or "I am calling at the suggestion of Mr. Smith." If your voice conveys uncertainty, you may be giving the secretary just cause to screen you out.

And, **never** try to deceive the secretary by saying, "I am a friend," or "it is a personal call." You will only alienate your prospect.

A secretary can be your best ally or your biggest stumbling block. Be sure to get his/her name and establish a friendly relationship. Remember, they have access to your target and are likely to share their impressions of you with the boss.

If you doubt that your target will return your call, indicate that you are going out and ask when might be a good time to call again. If after several calls, none have been returned, do not signal exasperation. This will make the secretary defensive. Instead, apologize for calling so often. Ask if you could schedule a phone appointment to break the cycle of telephone tag. The secretary may be moved by your respect for her time and either schedule a phone appointment, or provide you with information about a better time to call or, at least, push your message to the top of the pile.

If you cannot get the cooperation of the secretary, try calling before 9 a.m., after 5 p.m. or during lunch when your target person is more likely to answer his/her own phone. Busy lawyers are also likely to be in their offices on Saturdays.

Understand that it may take several attempts over a period of weeks—even months to get someone's attention. Keep in mind that the way to get a response to any kind of marketing communication is to create multiple, **positive** impressions.

YOU'RE READY FOR
AN INTERVIEW

When you can respond affirmatively to **all** of these statements, you are ready to proceed with informational interviewing.

___I can articulate my strength, skills, motives and goals.

___I am positive and upbeat and fully expect the meeting
   to be successful.

___I present myself in a professional manner.

___I dress in a way that projects a positive image.

___I am prepared to take charge of the meeting.

___I have specific questions to ask.

___I have prepared a list of target organizations and will
   readily ask for referrals.

8

THE INFORMATIONAL INTERVIEW

SETTING THE AGENDA

Once you are in your contact's office, it is your responsibility to lead the conversation. You should be prepared to:

- explain the purpose of the meeting
- show how your contact can be helpful
- present your background and skills to put the meeting in context
- ask questions to elicit the information you need
- give your contact a positive pleasant experience of you

- get the names of others who could be helpful
- be considerate of their time

The purpose of the meeting is to determine how your talents could be used in different settings, so it is important to do a good job presenting them. The ability to communicate your qualifications to employers entails more than just informing them of your technical competence. You must be able to illustrate that you have the requisite personal attributes—things like problem solving abilities, analytical skills, assessment and planning —to perform the job. The examples you use to talk about your accomplishments should demonstrate your thinking and problem solving style. The more concrete and specific you are, the better able your contact will be to think of possibilities for you and suggest additional people you should meet.

A common mistake people make during the networking/information gathering stage is to use the meeting as a therapy session. You do not want to inspire guilt, pity or dread. Your goal should be to make your contacts feel good about their ability to help you. It is important that you present yourself as positive, confident and self-assured, not negative, needy and desperate. Never make your contacts feel sorry for you or responsible for your situation. Do not scoff at their suggestions by saying "I've tried that and it does not work," otherwise your contacts will doubt their ability to help and begin to avoid you. If you need to express anger, bitterness, anxiety, etc., talk to a counselor or seek out a member of the clergy or a sympathetic friend before meeting with your contacts.

During your appointment you may want to address:

A. The career of the person you are visiting:
   - their background
   - how their interest developed in this area
   - what they like best/least about their work
   - their "career steps" (what former jobs they held, what they learned from each, how they progressed from one job to the next)

B. Advantages and disadvantages of work with:
   - that type of firm, agency or corporation
   - that type of law practice
   - that geographical area

C. What their organization is like and how it operates:
- who they supervise, and who they report to
- performance expectations
- advancement opportunities
- future growth potential

D. What organizations such as theirs are looking for in an employee.

E. What you could do to make yourself more attractive as a potential employee including:
- suggestions on upgrading your resume
- suggestions on interviewing techniques
- suggestions on additional educational and experiential qualifications you might pursue
- suggestions on where to go to find more information
- suggestions of others in the field with whom you could speak

G. Do they know of any specific job openings you should consider?

Once the individual gets to know you, and you have asked questions about their career (showing genuine interest), it is their prerogative to offer further assistance. Towards the conclusion of your talk, their thoughts might naturally turn to what action they might take on your behalf.

You should express gratitude for offers of assistance and take notes if the individual suggests that you contact colleagues. You might add, "Would it be OK if I use your name when contacting this person?" If your contact offers to send out your resumes for you or make calls on your behalf, make sure you arrange to get a list of those contacted so that you can take control of the follow-up process. Assuming responsibility for the follow-up process will allow your contact to experience you as efficient and conscientious.

Should your contact not offer assistance or additional names of people to call, you might gently ask if they could suggest names of individuals to speak to who could give you more information.

You may find that the 15 minutes you asked for stretched to a conversation lasting an hour or more. This usually occurs because the individual is flattered that you came to them for advice, and are asking about things of importance to them. However, it's up to **you** to stick to your preset time limit, and let your contact take the initiative to extend the meeting, if he so desires.

People love to talk about themselves. This type of conversation tends to be very warm and animated, filled with good will. Even though they do not know of a specific job opening, your contacts are likely to keep you in mind when they do have one, or when a colleague is trying to fill a position, they may recommend you to them.

When you meet with people on your network list, take notes about the meeting. It would be helpful to start a file for each contact. Whether you choose a sophisticated computer software program or a simple 3 x 5 index card filing system, be sure to include:

- the contact's name (be sure you have the correct spelling)
- the date of the contact
- the results of the meeting
- follow-up that is required and the time frame
- the person who referred you
- any personal information that may be helpful
- your impressions of the person and the organization

The job search process requires that you continually make phone calls, schedule appointments, write follow-up notes, contact new people, etc. It is important to record the dates and times for each activity on a pocket calendar to remind you what needs to be done. This will help to organize your days which in turn will allow you to get more accomplished.

FOLLOW-UP CORRESPONDENCE

People who help you should be kept apprised of your job search. If a lead they provide results in an interview, let them know. Keep people informed. A note every two or three months is appropriate. Remember, the way to get a response to any kind of marketing communication is to create multiple, positive impressions. **Your** job search may not be the most important thing on your contact's mind. If you occasionally can remind people that you are still in the job search, other opportunities may present themselves down the line.

After each informational interview, review your performance. Did you present your skills as effectively as possible? Did you craft your questions to elicit the information you needed? What could you have done better?

Organize the information you have received. Are there new books to read, new resources to consider, additional organizations to explore, new people to meet?

Develop your plan of action based on this new information.

Send a thank you letter and reference specific follow-up action planned. As a general rule, thank-you notes should be typed, particularly if you want to be more formal or if you have terrible handwriting. Handwritten notes are fine if you have a prior relationship with the person or if the meeting was brief and informal.

It is appropriate to recontact people as you go through the process. New information may generate new questions. Additionally, your contact may be interested to learn some of the information you have uncovered.

Informational interviewing requires a long-term view, strategic planning and a commitment to working at it. It takes patience and perseverance to use this process to uncover job opportunities, but the payoff can be enormous.

9

ANSWERING CLASSIFIED ADS AND USING HEADHUNTERS

In addition to job prospecting and informational interviewing, scanning the classified ads should be a routine part of your job search. However, as mentioned earlier, studies show that no more than 25% of placements occur through formal mechanisms such as answering ads. While this is an important job search activity, consider how long the process will take if you spend 100% of your time focused on only 25% of the market. It is worthwhile to respond to ads only if:

- the position advertised suits you particularly well and you are in the ballpark of the stated requirements

- you are doing all you can to uncover opportunities through informal methods and want to use spare hours productively

Respond immediately after the ad appears and plan to send a second letter 10 to 14 days later. Do not mention your previous correspondence. The idea behind the second letter is that if you are not already on the short list of people to be interviewed, the second letter, which will arrive after the first rush of applications, may get your name added.

Remember to utilize your contacts. Do any of them work at this organization? Might they know someone who does? Do not make the assumption that because you met with a contact months ago that they will remember that you are still in a job search and will automatically think of you for the position. Use this as an opportunity to reconnect with your contacts and remind them that you are still seeking new opportunities.

Always send a letter along with your resume as well as any supporting materials you believe will enhance your candidacy. In your letter, identify the source of the ad and outline the defined and implied qualifications in the advertisement showing how you meet or surpass the qualifications. The goal of your packet is to entice the reader to want to meet you.

Many ads these days request salary information. Sometimes employers will raise the question so early on in order to speed the process of plowing through a mountain of resumes and cover letters, even if that means missing out on some talented people. The salary question is the area that causes job seekers the greatest anxiety. Job seekers need to decide whether they prefer to risk being prematurely screened out by committing to a salary range up front or by ignoring the question altogether. Either approach is a gamble.

You may want to try to give a broad range, based on your research as well as on the information you uncovered during your networking meetings. A local executive recruiter or your college/law school career planning center also can offer you valuable guidance.

The key to answering the salary question is to understand the question behind the question, and then, using your lawyering skills, to restate the question into one you want to answer. Never simply state a number devoid of a narrative.

Instead of writing:

- "My salary requirement is between $70,000 and $90,000," or

- "My current salary is $87,000,"

Try instead:

- "Based on my research, I understand that a position such as the one described pays in the range of $70,000 to $90,000. I would appreciate the opportunity to meet with you to discuss how my qualifications could meet your needs."

- "While a comparable position in the private sector might pay over $150,000 as compared with $60,000 - $85,000 in the public sector, the added bonus of working within such a collegial and challenging environment makes this position very attractive to me."

See Chapter 12 for more information on salaries.

Concentrate on ads with company names listed. Call the company to find out the name of the person responsible for hiring. The applicant with a proper salutation will be noticed by employers. The effort illustrates a keen interest in the position because the applicant put time and effort into investigating the organization. If you can not uncover a name, address your letter "Good Morning" instead of "Dear Recruiter" or "Dear Sir/Madam" or "Dear Sirs". Not only does it sound more upbeat, there is also less chance of offending the reader.

Try to determine what department the opening is in and send a separate resume to the head of that department as well. Refer to the ad and indicate that you have already responded to it and are taking this opportunity to introduce yourself personally.

BLIND ADS

"Blind ads" or "confidential listing" are used for a variety of reasons. Employers may not want employees to know a position will be created or someone will be fired or an employment agency trying to increase its pool of applicants may place a fake ad. Either way, these types of ads are frustrating to job searchers because it makes it much more difficult to target your cover letter. Again, be creative. Call the post office representing the zip code in the ad. If the rental box application states it deals with the public, the name of the firm is public information and may be revealed by the post office. You can then do your homework about the organization.

Answering ads is **not** a passive job search activity. Job seekers would be well advised to keep copious notes about where and when applications were sent. Take control of the follow-up by using the telephone. Try saying:

> "I sent my resume last week and wanted to call to introduce myself and see if you need any other information from me at this point."

A simple conversation may help to uncover all sorts of information. Perhaps you will learn:

- the position has already been filled
- your resume was never received
- interviewing will not begin until next month
- information about the competition ("We received 400 resumes!")

Whatever the conversation reveals, the more information you have, the better able you will be to develop an appropriate response.

Understand and accept the fact that it may take several weeks for employers to respond to your application—if they respond at all. It is frustrating—it is rude—but it is life! Do not spend valuable energy fretting over non-responses. Use your energy to follow-up on applications. Be careful not to allow your frustration to affect the tone and content of your phone calls. You want to convey the attitude of "How can I help you with the onerous task of selecting candidates to interview?" and **not** "How dare you not recognize my qualifications and want to meet me!"

HEADHUNTER/EXECUTIVE RECRUITERS

Law firms do not rely on headhunters as heavily as they once did. They tend to utilize headhunters when they have an immediate and specific need. Candidates who come to employers via headhunters come with a huge price tag attached (usually 1/3 of the candidates first year salary!) which is why headhunters generally do not work with entry level attorneys. (Employers know they can contact schools directly and avoid the fee.) Candidates who use their contacts to stay in the loop and uncover openings can approach employers directly, eliminate the headhunter's fee and make themselves a more attractive candidate.

With that said, it is still important for job hunters to learn how to incorporate headhunters into their job search activities. Because it is the headhunters business to know what is happening in the marketplace, they can provide valuable information about things like which academic and professional credentials are hot and which geographic regions have increasing legal opportunities. Because of the volatile nature of the legal market, long term careers with one employer are extremely rare. By maintaining ties with those in the know, you may be able to stay one step ahead of the changes.

Refer to the annual pull-out sections of the *American Lawyer* or the *Legal Times* for names of executive recruiters. Listed by geographic location, these publications provide information about the company's size, number of attorney placements made and other important information. You may also want to contact the National Association of Legal Search Consultants. And, by all means, if a recruiter calls you, **take the call**! Keep an open mind at least long enough to hear the pitch and see what you can learn.

Before you decide to proceed with a headhunter, ask what procedures will be followed as well as what precautions will be taken to ensure your privacy and maintain the confidentiality of all transactions. Similarly, if you learn of an opening independently, do not let the headhunter send your resume. Send it yourself and avoid having the price tag attached to your application.

Generally, the process follows a similar pattern. First, you will be interviewed by the headhunter to determine what you are looking for and if any suitable positions currently exist. If so, you will be asked for your permission to send your resume to the employer. The headhunter's task is to present your credentials in such a way as to entice the employer to want to meet you. Once that is accomplished, you can expect multiple interviews with the employer. If the employer determines that you are the candidate he wants to hire, you will begin salary negotiations through the headhunter. It is important to remember that the fee-paying employer is the headhunter's "client" while you are merely the "candidate." **The headhunter always works for the client.**

Do not work with more than 2 or 3 headhunters at a time. Employers may list openings with several headhunters. If your resume lands on an employer's desk from several sources you risk looking desperate and destroying your candidacy by having a fee war develop over who sent your resume first.

Finally, remember that only about 10% of all job seekers obtain a new position by using headhunters. Allocate your time accordingly.

RESOURCES OF CURRENT
JOB OPENINGS FOR ATTORNEYS

In addition to classified ads in alumni newsletters, community newspapers and the local legal press, be sure to review:

- Access: Opportunities in Public Interest Law
- Association of American Law Schools Placement Bulletin
- Attorney Placement Bulletin
- Chronicle of Higher Education
- Chronicle of Philanthropy
- Cornerstone - National Legal Aid and Defenders Association
- International Employment Opportunities
- Job Market Previews (Civil Legal Services)
- National Business and Employment Weekly
- National & Federal Legal Employment Report
- Opportunities in Public Affairs
- Opportunities in Public Interest Law
- The Position Report
- Public Interest Advocate
- PIES (Public Interest Employment Service) Job Alert

10

MARKETING TOOLS: LEGAL RESUMES AND COVER LETTERS

THE RESUME

A resume is an opportunity to create a positive impression with an employer. It may be viewed as a photograph that presents a certain image, yet leaves a more compelling story to be told—perhaps during an interview. Because this document is a self-portrait, it is sometimes difficult to give generic advice on the preparation of a legal resume. Yet, there are key concepts and general rules of thumb to follow concerning format and content.

- **A resume should be limited to one page**—however, if you have had an extensive career and need to expand to another page, remember, the second page should be at least half full and repeat your name, address and telephone number at the top of the page. When in doubt, stick to a one page resume unless you are a very senior level attorney.

- **Name, address and phone number should appear at the top of the resume**—phone numbers are essential; invest in an answering machine to avoid missed opportunities.

- **No job objective is necessary** on a legal resume.

- **Experience** section can be formatted either **Chronologically** or **Functionally**. **Chronological resumes** are oriented by date, with the most recent position first and proceeding backward. This is the most popularly used and accepted format because it is logical and easy to follow. This is the format to use if you have a steady work history with no gaps and if your most recent job is related to your job target. If this is not the case a **functional resume** may be more effective. Here accomplishments and experience are organized under broad skills or practice area headings with the most important category at the top, followed by two or three other functions. This format allows you to organize your experience according to your interests. It also allows you to de-emphasize employment dates, company names and titles.

- **Education section should contain all pertinent information from your law school experience,** including the official name of the school, year of graduation, Journal/Moot Court experience and a list of any appropriate academic and/or extra-curricular activities. This section should also contain similar information for other graduate schools attended as well as your undergraduate institution. Generally your education goes **after** experience on a legal resume once you have had at least one year of professional experience. If you had stellar grades in law school, you may want to keep your education section first for your first year or two after graduation.

- **Consider including a section which draws attention to unique skills such as foreign languages, computer skills, and any personal interests.** The section may be titled

Personal or **Interests**. Its purpose is to facilitate conversation or "break the ice" during an interview and to give the employer a more well rounded appreciation of your background. Make sure that your personal interests are descriptive—i.e., "travel to the Far East, Mexican cooking and nineteenth century literature" are much more effective than "travel, reading and cooking."

- **Consider adding a section for Professional Affiliations and/or Community Activities.** This will enable you to list bar association committees, board memberships, pro bono work, and any other extra-curricular or leadership positions on your resume.

- **Include CLE or other continuing legal education courses or symposia under a Continuing Legal Education section.** This can be useful to include if you are trying to make a transition to a different practice area. You can demonstrate knowledge of and an interest in a particular field by listing this type of course work on your resume.

- **Legal Resumes should generally be conservative in appearance.** White, off- white or cream colored heavy stock paper should be used. No photos or other graphics are necessary. Ten, eleven or twelve point print size is appropriate. As much as you may be tempted to stand out from the pack, the legal profession is conservative, and flashy "ploys" are not usually well received. Good fonts include **Times** and **Helvetica**. Try to do your resume on a home computer so you can quickly adjust it for different jobs.

- **No Personal Information (height, weight, age, marital status, health)** need appear on your resume.

- **Prepare a List of References** that is separate from your resume. It is not typical on a legal resume to include names of references. Prepare a separate sheet of paper listing references (three is usually an adequate number) to have available when you go for an interview. Use paper which matches your resume and cover letter. Don't forget to alert your references first so they are prepared for a potential employer's call. Phone references are usually preferred over written references.

Other tips and techniques to keep in mind:

- **Use CAPITALIZATION, bold print, <u>underlining</u>, indentation and outline format** to present information. Make the resume easy to scan.

- **Use CAPITALIZATION, bold lettering and white space** around an item, such as your name, to help the reader remember the item.

- Use generous margins (but not so generous as to look skimpy!).

- **Laser Print** your resume if at all possible! Do not use a dot matrix or other type of printer unless the print is perfectly clear and smudge free.

- Put dates on the right hand margin instead of the left so they do not stand out to the point that the employer will be distracted from the more important aspects of your resume.

- Use "bullets" if your descriptions are longer than 5 lines.

- Make sure the overall look is neat and clean.

- Balance text on the page.

- **Proofread to eliminate errors and typos!** Do not rely on yourself to proofread your own resume—you will miss errors because you have become too familiar with it.

Think of your resume as a sales document. To design an effective sales document, you must have a clear idea of the job you are seeking so that you can skew your resume to your target audience. Concentrate on format and style as well as content. Decide which information to include; pay close attention to the words you use to describe your experiences.

Consider starting your resume with a **Biographical Summary** consisting of several statements that demonstrate your credentials or that you are a perfect fit for the position. The focus is on your abilities.

Describe what you **can** do, not what you **want** to do.

Another option is a **Career Summary** paragraph highlighting your professional background as it relates to the desired position.

Another choice includes beginning your resume with a paragraph entitled **Professional Capabilities** allows you to list what you have done as well as what you think you can do in the future.

Use the sample resume formats on pages 99-101 to structure your resume and the form on page 102 to critique your final product. We've also included samples of completed resumes in the Appendix (pages 173-184). You should examine these for tips on how you can best write your own resume.

SAMPLE RESUME (Experienced Attorney)

Name
Address
Phone

BAR STATUS

Admitted in New Jersey and Connecticut (or) Passed New York State; awaiting admission.

LEGAL EXPERIENCE

Employer Name	City, State
<u>Your Title</u>	Dates
Description. Use action verbs!	

Employer Name	City, State
<u>Your Title</u>	Dates
Description. Use action verbs!	

ADDITIONAL EXPERIENCE

Employer Name	City, State
<u>Your Title</u>	Dates
Description. Use action verbs!	

EDUCATION

School Name
J.D., May 1983
Class Standing: Top 1/3
Honors:
Activities:

School Name
B.A., Economics May 1979
G.P.A.: 3.7
Honors:
Activities:

LANGUAGES:

Fluent in Spanish; working knowledge of German.

PERSONAL:

Interests include spy novels, cross-county skiing and hockey.

References Available Upon Request

SAMPLE RESUME (Functional resume)

NAME

Current Address   Permanent Address
Street   Street
City, State Zip   City, State, Zip
Phone   Phone

SKILLS (or **PRACTICE AREAS**)

Research: (Securities)

Writing: (Trusts & Estates)   (Give a brief description of what you have done
                                     in each of these areas, drawing from all of your
                                     experiences.)

Negotiating: (Corporate)

Presentation: (Tax)

Management: (Financial Services)

EMPLOYMENT HISTORY

Employer Name, Your title, dates
Employer Name, Your title, dates
Employer Name, Your title, dates

EDUCATION

School Name
J.D. 1985

School Name
B.A., cum laude, 1980

COMMUNITY ORGANIZATIONS

Member, Parent/Teacher Association
President, St. Mary's Parish Council

References Available Upon Request

SAMPLE RESUME (Recent Graduate)

NAME

> Address
> Home Phone

BAR STATUS

Admitted in New Jersey and Connecticut (or) Passed New York State; awaiting admission

EDUCATION

School Name
J.D., May 1991
G.P.A.: 3.3

Honors:
> Associate Editor, *Fordham Urban Law Journal* (Journal membership can also be listed under activities)
> Dean's List
> American Jurisprudence Award

Activities:
> Black Law Students Association
> Fordham Public Service Project

School Name
B.A., *cum laude*, May 1990

Major:	Minor:
English	Computer Science

Honors:
> (list here)

Activities:
> (list here)

LEGAL EXPERIENCE

Employer Name	City, St
Your title	Dates

- Using bullets, describe your experience. Remember, use action verbs!

Employer Name	City, St
Your title	Dates

- Using bullets, describe your experience. Remember, use action verbs!

ADDITIONAL EXPERIENCE

Employer Name	City, St
Your title	Dates

- Using bullets, describe your experience. Remember, use action verbs!

PERSONAL: Interests include English literature, Giants football and golf

References Available Upon Request

RESUME SELF-CRITIQUE FORM

Use the following form as a way to judge your own resume before sending it out.

	Excellent	Satisfactory	Needs Work
OVERALL APPEARANCE Attractive, interesting/compelling			
LAYOUT Looks professional, well typed and printed, good margins, use of white space, caps, headings			
MARKETING Key sales points stand out			
RELEVANCE Extraneous material has been eliminated			
WRITING STYLE Well-written, making it easy to get a picture of the candidate's qualifications			
ACTION ORIENTATION All sentences and paragraphs start with strong skill verbs in the past tense			
SPECIFICITY Resume avoids generalities and focuses on specific information about experience, projects, products and quantifies with numbers/percentages when possible			
ACCOMPLISHES Candidate's accomplishments and problem-solving skills emphasized			
COMPLETENESS All important information is covered			
BOTTOM LINE Resume accomplishes its ultimate purpose of getting the employer to invite the applicant in for an interview			
ESSENTIALS Candidate has included address, phone numbers, bar admissions and year of Law School graduation			
COMMENTS AND ADDITIONAL WAYS TO IMPROVE THIS RESUME:			

COVER LETTERS

An individual cover letter must accompany each resume you send out. Its purpose is to support your candidacy by supplementing the information set forth in your resume. A cover letter should:

- Convince the reader that you are worth getting to know better.
- Draw attention away from liabilities by addressing potential questions the resume may raise.
- Emphasize salient achievements and accomplishments in greater depth than the resume does.
- Introduce new sales material that is not included on your resume.
- Demonstrate enthusiasm and knowledge of the industry.

A cover letter is the ideal place to focus on the specific skills you want to emphasize for a particular employer. Some general guidelines for writing good cover letters include:

- Use correct grammar, good sentence structure and standard business letter format. Use paper that matches your resume.

- State the purpose of your letter. If you are responding to an ad, indicate the source. If you are writing at the suggestion of a mutual acquaintance, indicate that immediately. If you are writing about the possibility of a job, indicate why you are writing to this particular organization. Cover letters should be slanted as individually as possible.

- Pinpoint how your skills and experience relate to the particular needs of the employer to whom you are writing. Focus your letter on the needs of the reader. Focus on what **you** can do for the employer (what credentials, skills and experience do you have that would help the employer), not what the job would do for you.

- Always be objective when describing yourself to an employer. For example, instead of writing "I am a hard worker," "I would be a great asset to your firm," or "I have many leadership qualities," show them by means of examples from your past: "The experience I gained as director of the office is indicative of my leadership abilities."

- Address your letter to a specific person by name and title. (It's always smart to call and double check, as hiring partners change frequently).

- Do some research on the organization before writing your letter. Read annual reports or brochures, look the organization up on Lexis or Westlaw, use the information you learn in your informational interviews, or if you have an understanding of the field, ask yourself what kinds of problems this particular employer is likely to be facing.

- Limit your cover letter to three or four paragraphs. It should rarely be more than one page.

- Present unique or distinctive attributes, without using super-latives, in an attractive, professional and well written manner.

- Close your cover letter with a request for an interview in-dicating what action you will take—i.e., that you will call them (within 7 - 10 days) to arrange a meeting. Then follow through.

- Keep careful records of the positions for which you have ap-plied. Maintain copies of your correspondence with dates indicating when you will follow-up. FOLLOW-UP is crucial.

SAMPLE COVER LETTER

Your name
Street Address
City, State zip
Date

Employer Name
Title
Organization
Street Address
City, State, Zip

Dear:

First paragraph: Mention the name of any person who referred you to this employer **first**, if this information is available to include. Otherwise, start your letter with a powerful statement that will grab the reader's attention. Identify yourself and the type of position you are seeking. State how you heard about this job opening. ("As an attorney with 15 years experience in the prosecutor's office, I am writing in response to your advertisement in the New York Times for litigators.")

Second paragraph: Explain why you are qualified for or interested in this particular position. Stress how **you** can benefit the employer and what **you** have to offer. Don't repeat word-for-word the text of your resume. Rather, highlight and embellish upon the most significant aspects of your background with regard to the particular employer. Consider using bullets to draw attention to your accomplishments.

Third paragraph: Restate your interest in the particular organization, and express your desire for an interview. State how the employer may contact you if your address and phone number are **different** from the information on your resume. You may also state that you will call to set up an appointment. If you are truly interested in this job, feel free to take the initiative.

Sincerely,

Type your name

Enclosure

11

SELLING YOUR PRODUCT: JOB INTERVIEWS

ESTABLISHING GOALS AND OBJECTIVES

The time spent preparing for an interview is time well spent. You are now ready to sell your "product" to a prospective employer.

While it is unlikely to be posed directly, the basic question in every interview is "Why should I hire you?" You need to be able to translate your skills and attributes into benefits for the employer. You must be able to verbalize why your strengths are of value to this specific employer. Do not expect your past experience to speak for itself.

The recruiter's objective is to assess your credentials, form an impression about your personality and determine the degree to which your interests and background correspond with the employer's hiring needs. Your background and record of accomplishments are amplified or diminished in the eyes of the recruiter by the general impression you create. Decision makers base choices on generally favorable impressions:

- do you interact with people easily?
- are you easy to interview, confident and clear in your answers?
- do you listen?
- do you ask sensible questions?
- are you likeable?
- do you "fit in" with the environment?

Given that the recruiter will be meeting more than a dozen people, it is clear that it is the prepared, articulate candidate who will make a favorable impression and stand out in the recruiters mind.

Obtain information about the employer from as many sources as possible. Knowing about things like areas of practice and client bases enables you to formulate intelligent questions. You do not want to waste valuable time asking questions that can easily be answered by reading the employer's brochure. The more information you have before the interview the better you will be able to make a convincing connection between your skills and the employer's needs.

STRATEGIES FOR OVERCOMING BARRIERS

Some of the major obstacles to overcome in the interview process include:

- anxiety, nervousness
- lack of confidence
- lack of practice in interviewing
- intimidation
- untrained or unskilled recruiters
- lack of information and inadequate preparation

To overcome these barriers, you should try to focus on your message instead of on your nerves. Remember, you would not be approaching this meeting at all if you were not qualified for the position. Interviewing is akin to developing an oral argument; present your qualifications based on the evidence you uncovered during the process of self-assessment.

The first four minutes of the interview are crucial. Employers make up their mind about candidates very early. Your handshake must be firm and confident, your gaze steady, your appearance impeccable and your confidence apparent.

Your thorough preparation will make you aware of both your strengths and your weaknesses. But remember, the interviewer is there to see what you **have** to offer, not to hear explanations about what you don't have. When you practice answering interview questions, eliminate all "no's," "not's," "didn't's," "although," "buts," and "howevers" from your speech. Rephrase your answers using positive speech forms. This will prepare you to speak about yourself in a positive light.

Think of at least three main points you want to make. Use concrete and clear examples that demonstrate these strengths. Focus on these identified strengths during the interview and present them with conviction and enthusiasm. Remember that the interviewer must be able to see and hear the enthusiasm that you wish to convey.

Try to anticipate the types of questions you will be asked and prepare multi-level responses. Write out your answers. Review and edit them. First, give a **brief** summary, akin to a verbal outline, covering all salient points. Second, pause and give a more detailed description **if the interviewer seems interested** or asks you to go on. Be certain that your responses highlight your skills and abilities; demonstrate your knowledge and expertise and reflect your motivation and personality.

There can be many goals and objectives in the interview process. Some of these include:

- to relate successes and achievements, to inform, to represent yourself and to convey an image of intelligence, integrity, responsiveness, responsibility and achievement-orientation
- to convey conscientiousness, reliability, and a capacity for hard work
- to develop rapport, to be liked, to have a pleasant conversation, to make a favorable impression
- to distinguish yourself from the competition
- to investigate employment opportunities and other important factors (i.e., amount of responsibility, training, exposure to clients, nature of tasks, supervision, advancement, pro bono support, satisfaction level of coworkers, method of work assignment, specialty areas, prospects for firm growth and development). You want to learn if this will be a good fit.

To meet these goals you **must**:

1. **Establish rapport**—In addition to tangible things such as a good, firm handshake and appropriate eye contact, there are additional items which develop rapport between people. These include friendliness and sincere interest in the interviewer, as well as warmth and responsiveness to the interviewer. You must become aware of body language. Be sensitive to cues of boredom. If the interviewer keeps looking down at your resume or out the window, bring the statement you are making to a close.

2. **Listen carefully**—Try to hear the question behind the question and respond to the interviewer's concerns. Get the interviewer to talk about the position to uncover exactly what is being sought. This will enable you to illustrate how you can fill these needs.

3. **Ask questions**—Remember, this is a conversation; there should be interaction. Ask technical questions to demonstrate your knowledge of the field and to show that you are already looking for solutions to the employer's problems. **Do not** ask about benefits, vacations, pensions and hours until you know you have an offer.

4. **Get feedback**—Before the end of the interview, ask if you have the qualifications they are seeking. If not, now is the best time to find out so you can adjust your approach.

5. **Take control of the follow-up process**—When interviewers indicate they will "let you know," imply that because you will be out networking and interviewing, you might be difficult to contact. Ask if you can call on a specific day. This will help to accelerate the decision-making process.

   The most effective follow-up is initiated by telephone, however, a letter is also acceptable. The purpose of your follow-up is to reinforce the employer's understanding of your value. You will want to:

   ▪ provide new information that was not available at the time of the interview

- clarify any confusing information with which you may have left the employer
- convey a sense of urgency. Let the employer know you are moving quickly, considering other job offers and wanting to proceed with other prospects.

6. **Most importantly, have a positive attitude!** Adopt a "have done - can do - will do" attitude. It is not always what you say that counts but **how** you say it. View anything negative as a challenge, an opportunity, and something exciting. Do not be apologetic about anything; handle your "Achilles' Heel" factually and non-defensively.

You can help an inexperienced interviewer feel more comfortable by asking questions. Your prepared questions can demonstrate your knowledge of the field and your interest in the employer and provide the interviewer with an opportunity to relax by talking about something with which he/she is familiar. You can ask things like:

- "From my research I discovered that you are involved in the (i.e., Labor) area. How did you get interested in this area?"
- "What do you see as the growth areas of the firm?"
- "What departments are likely to do well in the next few years?"

By offering questions that allow the interviewer to relax and think about the answers, the interview becomes a freer exchange of information, which benefits all the parties involved. The interviewer will feel more comfortable in your presence and will be more likely to recommend you to the hiring committee.

EXERCISE

PLANNING THE INTERVIEW

Provide answers to the following questions.

1. What is my strategy for the interview? What are the three points I must make at some time during our conversation?

2. What are my most marketable skills, both legal and management?

3. What are the skills I most want to use in my next job?

4. What are the aspects (tendencies, interview abilities, comfort level, specific questions I am nervous about being asked) of the interview situation on which I most need to work? What is the question I am most afraid of being asked?

INTERVIEWING STYLES

Understanding the differences between the four major interviewing styles and preparing a strategy to effectively deal with each of them will also improve your chances for success:

1. **Directive Interview:** short, precise questions designed to elicit specific information about your background and interests are asked. The questions are formulated from the contents of your resume. **Strategy:** Answers should be brief and should objectively emphasize concrete accomplishments. Be careful to be concise but do not fall into the trap of responding with monosyllabic yes or no answers.

2. **Non-Directive Interview:** The recruiter's intent is to get the candidate to do all the talking. This usually does not work to your advantage. Your goal should be to get the recruiter to do at least 50% of the talking. **Strategy:** Construct a narrative history of yourself in advance to enable you to make a clear concise statement explaining your purpose at the interview. Attempt to draw the recruiter into the conversation by asking questions.

3. **Stress Interview:** This is perhaps the most difficult interview of all. Its purpose is to measure your poise and emotional stability. The recruiter tries to appear curt, argumentative and/or impatient, firing questions in rapid succession. The questions may be designed to annoy you or bait you into a topical argument. **Strategy:** Remain patient and calm. Indicating annoyance, tension or nervousness serves no purpose. To avoid a debate, try to change the topic by asking a question. Remember, this type of interview is designed to rattle you.

4. **Free-Wheeling Interview:** This type of interview lacks any semblance of structure or direction. Since many attorneys have limited interviewing experience, they have no tactical plan. **Strategy:** Control the flow of the conversation by opening the interview with highlights of your accomplishments and then move directly into your own questions. This helps put the recruiter at ease and helps to focus him/her on your assets.

QUESTIONS INTERVIEWERS ASK

It may help you focus your thoughts if you **write down** responses to the following questions. This is to help you strategize. Do not try to memorize these as responses. If you do, they will almost certainly sound "canned." Your responses don't have to be long—just a few sentences each:

1. Tell me about yourself. (what they're really asking here is, "What in your background makes you a good candidate for this job?" This is not the time for an autobiography)

2. What are your long range and short range goals and objectives? (be sure to make the connection between your goals and this job for which you're interviewing)

3. What do you see yourself doing five years from now? (again, tie your answer into the position available. Never, ever say you want to be doing something unrelated!)

4. What made you decide to go to law school? (show your commitment to the legal profession)

5. Why should I hire you?

6. What two or three accomplishments have given you the most satisfaction? Why?

7. In what ways do you think you can make a contribution to our firm/company?

8. In what sort of environment are you most comfortable? (ideally, your favorite environment will be similar to the employer's with whom you are interviewing. Find this information out by conducting thorough research.)

9. Why do you want to work with our agency/company/firm? (be specific. Show you've done your research!)

10. What do you consider to be the strongest qualities in your personality and character? (list about 3 and relate them to the job opening)

11. What are your greatest weaknesses? (be honest but not negative. Show how you turned a weakness into a strength or discuss a weakness that is unrelated to the position for which you are interviewing.)

12. I see from your resume that you _____ (play basketball **or** speak French **or** are interested in real estate, etc. This is **not** a statement where you answer "yes" or "no". Hear this as: **tell me more about** your basketball team or French speaking abilities or interest in real estate.)

13. What else do you think I should know about you? (from your preparation beforehand you will have an additional strength or accomplishment that you'll want to highlight here. Don't say there isn't anything else. You're more exciting than that!)

14. Do you have any questions that I can answer? (this usually signals that the interview is beginning to come to a close. Have several prepared questions that are good. **Don't ask anything about the employer that you could have found out by reading information that is publicly available**. Even inexperienced interviewers can spot a canned or "recommended" question a mile away! In some way, personalize your questions, and make them **your own**. Some suggestions follow.)

SUGGESTED QUESTIONS TO ASK INTERVIEWERS

1. From my research, I see that you are involved in the (i.e., Tax) area. Could you tell me how you got interested in this area and a little bit about what your practice is like?

2. What kind of responsibilities would an associate be assigned?

3. What do you see as the overall growth areas of the firm/ company?

4. What departments are likely to expand in the next few years?

5. I was particularly interested to learn about _____, but you have really covered that information quite extensively. (Restate what you learned)

You may want to raise this issue if you believe negative assumptions are being made about you, confidently address the issue in order to eliminate the perceptions.

6. During other interviews, I have been asked about (my ability to accept supervision from someone younger than me, or about my child care arrangements or my commitment to this geographic area) and we haven't talked about that yet.

Your questions should not convey concern over salary or time off or any of the more mundane aspects of the job. Stay interested in important aspects such as challenge, responsibility, and those which show a mature and forward-thinking mentality. The dollars and cents concerns can be ironed out after an offer has been made.

ADDITIONAL POINTS TO REMEMBER

- Establish your connection to out-of-town cities for out-of-town employers.
- Be yourself.
- Feel free to pause when framing an answer.
- Never say anything negative about anything! It always ends up reflecting back onto **you**, and **you** will be remembered as a negative person.
- Be especially enthusiastic for later in the day (after 3:00 pm) interviews.
- It's O.K. to say "I'm not sure of the answer to that."
- You're interviewing the employer as much as he/she is interviewing you!

AVOIDING DISCRIMINATORY QUESTIONS

Hiring decisions tend to be based on somewhat subjective material. Unfortunately, trying to determine if someone "fits in" to a particular environment can lead to subtle forms of discrimination. While interviewers usually try to avoid asking personal questions, most want to know all they can about the applicants. Help them by providing information that you are comfortable with discussing and would like the interviewer to know. The information you volunteer about yourself will be different from what every other applicant offers and will help you stand out in the crowd. A word of caution: do not allow yourself to be lured into intimate chit-chat. Regardless of the kindness of the interviewer, **nothing** is "off the record." Keep your comments job related and, if you can complement your resume in any way by adding something, do it!

Applicants who are not aware of what questions should and should not be asked are more likely to be victims of discrimination. The general rule of thumb is, if the information is not specifically job related, it should not be asked. Examples of potentially sensitive subjects include:

- name
- residence
- age
- birthplace
- military service
- references
- national origin
- sex
- marital status
- family size

- race
- color
- physical description
- physical condition
- photograph
- religion
- arrest record
- criminal record
- fraternal membership

Each of these subjects has many variations, which adds to the complexity of the problem. Asking "Are you a U.S. Citizen?" or "Where were you born?" is different from asking you "Are you authorized to work in the U.S.?" Similarly, while it is acceptable for an employer to inquire "Are you willing to relocate?" it is not acceptable for him/her to attempt to infer the answer to that by asking "Are you married?"

In most states there are laws that render some questions illegal. Employers are advised **not** to ask an applicant:

- if he/she has worked under another name

- the maiden name of wife or mother

- to take a physical examination or to inquire about the nature and severity of physical or mental handicaps prior to making an offer

- about marital plans, arrangements for child care, current or anticipated pregnancy status

- about the occupations of spouses, parents or siblings

- for information relating to family background that may reveal race, ethnicity, religion, citizenship and/or national origin

- about holidays observed or membership in clubs, churches and fraternities

- about languages written, spoken or read unless the employer is specifically seeking to hire someone with that particular skill or it is listed on your resume

- for proof of age

- for a photograph **prior** to the interview

When you suspect an interviewer has lured you into a dangerous area, you have several response options.

1. You could answer the question. Realize, however, that you are providing information that is not job related and you risk harming your candidacy by responding "incorrectly."

2. You could refuse to answer the question. While you are in your rights to do so, you will probably alienate the employer and come across as uncooperative, confrontational and hostile. Not exactly the ideal description of a desirable applicant.

3. You could examine the intent of the question, in other words, you could try to hear the question behind the question. For example, is the employer asking about your birthplace because there is a concern about your social status or is it because the interviewer grew up in the same place and is simply trying to make small talk.

Avoid becoming angry, hostile or argumentative. Calmly examine the clumsily expressed question to uncover the underlying concerns of the interviewer. For example, an employer who questions a woman if she is married or about her plans to have children. The employer is not really interested in the candidate's personal life, but rather is most probably attempting to learn how committed the candidate is to the job. You may answer such a question effectively by saying, "I am assuming by your question that you are concerned with whether or not I will be able to spend long hours at the office required to get the work done. I'd like to reassure you by mentioning that throughout law school, I held a full-time job, did well in my classes, studied long hours in the library and was not held back in any way by child care responsibilities."

Do yourself—and the employer—a favor: interview as if everything depended on you. Walk in with a clear idea of two or three selling points you would like to express. Use the interviewer's questions to introduce those points and back them up with real-life examples. At the end of the interview, summarize your qualifications and articulate your interest and enthusiasm for the job. If you leave the interview having convinced the employer you have something to offer, your color, sex, age, disability, sexual preference, nationality, etc. will not stand in your way of landing the job that you want!

THANK YOU NOTES

It is appropriate to send a thank you note shortly after the interview. Your letter should be crafted to not only thank people for the time they spent with you and the information they provided, but also to restate your interest and clarify or highlight any pertinent information you want the employer to remember.

If you interviewed with more than one person, you could send a thank you note to each person, however, you ought to vary the letters to reflect a specific aspect of the conversation you had with each individual person. Do not send three or four people the exact same letter.

Another option would be to send one letter to either the most senior person or the person with whom you established the greatest rapport. In your letter, ask that person to extend your thanks to the other individuals (refer to them by name!)

Finally, try to avoid the temptation to interpret what the employer is thinking. Remember, lawyers are trained to not give away clues. Just because you do not hear from the employer the next day or even the next week, do not assume a rejection will follow. Selecting candidates is a slow, time-consuming process. While two weeks on your end of the telephone seems like an eternity, that same time frame seems like nothing to an employer. If three or four weeks have passed and you have not heard from the employer, feel free to call to "check on the status" of your application.

12

CLOSING
THE DEAL:
EVALUATING &
NEGOTIATING
JOB OFFERS

C andidates often are very excited when they finally receive an
offer. It feels wonderful to know that you are wanted and that the
long and sometimes frustrating job search is coming to a close.
In their enthusiasm, many candidates assume that the only options
available are to accept or decline the offer on the table. Many shudder at
the idea of negotiating for more.

Negotiating is nothing more than individuals working together to
arrive at a mutually beneficial agreement. If you do not negotiate up
front, you may be underpaid by several thousands of dollars over the
years. There is room for disagreement and disappointment as well as
negotiation and compromise.

How you negotiate will affect your relationship with the employer. Negotiating should not be viewed as adversarial or confrontational. Rather, it should be viewed as an opportunity to win the respect and admiration of employers because it allows you to demonstrate confidence in your own marketability. Unemployed job seekers in particular should keep this in mind because they have a tendency to diminish their own worth. Instead of assuming you have to "prove yourself to employers," remember to highlight your existing accomplishments which already "prove your worth." Think in terms of exchanging your talent and labor for cash and benefits. Confidence is an extremely important asset at this phase of the job hunt.

In this tight market, many legal employers feel they can maintain their ground on salary offers. As more qualified lawyers glut the market, many job seekers are willing to take lower salaries. If you decide to apply for a job that is beneath your salary history, be prepared to explain why.

A general rule regarding the discussion of salary is to never bring up the subject until an offer of employment has been made. The goal is to give yourself and the interviewer a chance to get to know one another. That way both of you will have a better idea of how flexible you are willing to be with salary negotiations. You want to ensure that you acquire enough information about the job so that you will be able to effectively communicate that you possess the necessary qualifications for the position. Your goal is to get the employer to invest enough time in you so that you can illustrate that:

- you have done your research on the firm/organization
- you expect to receive a salary appropriate for your level of qualifications and experience.
- you expect to be compensated on the basis of performance, not on past salary history.

The last point is particularly important. The pay differential in the legal profession is unlike almost any other profession. External factors such as geography, size of firm and type of practice, can account for a salary differential of more than $50,000!

The salary question can crop up at any time during the job hunt and it comes in many forms:

- What is your current salary?

- How much were you paid at your previous employer?

- What are your salary requirements?

- What is the lowest figure you would accept?

- How much do you think you are worth?

- Why should we pay you more than other 5th year associates?

Although **you** should never ask about the salary until you are offered the job, you must be prepared to discuss it whenever the **employer** raises the issue.

Should the salary question arise early in the interview process and you feel you do not have enough information about the position, try to deflect the question.

- "I am a bit unclear about the responsibilities of the position. Could you tell me a little more about...."

If you state a figure outside of the range the employer has in mind—either too high or too low—you risk having it used against you as an easy, objective screening device.

Note whether you have been asked to reveal your **salary history** or **salary requirements.** In other disciplines, **salary history** can illustrate if a candidate is moving up, laterally or down the corporate ladder. In such disciplines, salary can provide some gauge for level of expertise or it can explain frequent job changes. But because the wide disparity of salary ranges within the legal field is often based on something other than individual performance, salary history actually reveals very little. For example, an attorney moving from the private sector to the public sector may be prepared to take a 50% cut in pay. Does that mean he is working his way down the corporate ladder? Probably not. The reality is, employers do not care, per se, about how much money you make. They really only want to know if you have realistic expectations about what **this** job pays.

It is important to know what you are worth and know what employers are willing to pay for someone with your skills as well as what salary you are willing to accept. Be able to justify the salary you are requesting by providing supporting examples. Next, calculate an appropriate salary **range** for the position based a realistic assessment of what the market will command. Review annual salary surveys published by trade magazines and associations. *The American Lawyer* and *David J. White*

& Associates, Inc. Annual Salary Survey can be great resources in addition to your own networking contacts.

Understand that before interviewing candidates, employers have a **predetermined budget** in their mind for the salary that they would like to pay. This figure, of course, is most financially beneficial for them. Most employers have some flexibility to negotiate salary, particularly at the higher level positions but, contrary to popular belief, everything is NOT negotiable. Many employers have rigid pay systems. They try to keep salaries equitable within the organization by not paying anyone much above the norm. As the interview process progresses, the employer **may** consider altering the budget if impressed by a particular candidate. It may be at this point that they may ask you what your salary expectations are. You need to sense whether they are flexible and negotiate accordingly.

Because of the salary explosions in the 1980's, many lawyers today have unrealistic salary expectations and exaggerated notions of their worth to prospective employers. Your approach should always be **employer-centered** not **self-centered**. You must be able to describe your worth in relation to the employer's position which has already been defined. Employers do not care that you have $80,000 in school loans; they do not care that you have a mortgage and two kids in college. Those facts do not increase your worth to them.

It is important to negotiate from knowledge (about the going rate) and strength (articulating your qualifications) and not from need, greed or ego.

Most jobs come with a similar package of benefits, but this may be the place that employers have the most room to negotiate. Remember to consider additional benefits such as:

- Health, life, dental, optical, disability and malpractice insurance
- Insurance for dependents
- Paid sick leave
- Maternity/Parental leave
- Vacation
- Personal leave/personal days
- Educational leave
- Health leave to care for dependents
- Profit sharing
- Stock Options
- Expense accounts for client entertaining
- Dues to professional associations

- Travel reimbursement
- Fee sharing arrangements for clients generated
- Relocation costs
- Sabbaticals
- Professional conference costs
- Flextime work schedules
- Fitness center memberships
- Bar review courses

When a definite salary offer is made consider it for several moments before you respond, even if you are disappointed with the figure. Clarify the job responsibilities as you understand them. Focus on the high-level end requirements.

"Let me make sure I understand the responsibilities of the position. I would be expected to....Is there anything I have left out?" (Be sure to focus them on the value of the position as it relates to you.)

Before even stating the dollar amount you are seeking, try to get the employer to reveal his range first. Ask:

- What is the normal range in your organization for a position such as this?

- What would the range be for someone with my qualifications?

By getting the employer to state a range first, you can than place the top of his range into the bottom of yours. For example, if the employer's range is $60,000 - $80,000, your range should be $80,000 - $100,000. Be ready to articulate why you are worth the salary you are seeking.

If you cannot get the employer to reveal a figure first, try saying:

"From my research I learned that the range for fourth year associates in this city is ...."

Emphasize the level of skill and talent you bring to the table citing achievements, using statistics, comparisons, even testimonials to support your case. In other words, state your value. You need to translate the employer's benefit to paying you more money than the norm.

Throughout the negotiating process remember to constantly reinforce that you are excited about the offer and that you want to take this position, even if you are disappointed with the figure. You do not want this to be an argument, but rather a way that you can get to the place that you want to be so that you can accept the offer. Ask to think about the offer.

> "I am very excited about the offer. Can you tell me what your time frame for a reply is?"

It is common professional courtesy for employers to provide candidates with some time to consider an offer.

If you are unhappy with what has been offered, it is appropriate to come back with a counteroffer. The key is to emphasize the benefit to the employer for paying you more. Perhaps if the employer cannot meet your salary expectations, you may be able to convince the employer to give you credit for judicial clerkships, superior academic performance or past careers. Perhaps you can convince the employer to create a new position that would better accommodate your skills, interests and abilities as well as meet their needs. If all else fails, and you still really want the job, suggest renegotiating the salary 3, 6 or 9 months later. Demonstrate your confidence in your abilities by saying something like:

> "Let me prove I am worth this. I would be happy to come in at this salary if you could agree to review my performance in six months."

If you are waiting to hear from other employers, contact them immediately and let them know you have an offer and would like to clarify your application status before you make any decisions. A second offer in hand could enhance your bargaining power. However, never lie about having another offer. While it may work, it could backfire and create ill will if the employer finds out. When you compromise your integrity, you demean your value to others and yourself. Remember, the legal profession demands total integrity of its members.

It is important to know when to stop negotiating and start the job. Reaching common ground and setting the stage for mutual respect and cooperation may be more important than the few extra dollars you might be able to obtain. Having your priorities in place will help you decide which things you are willing to sacrifice in the negotiating process.

ACCEPTING THE OFFER

By using the "Business Plan approach," you have learned how to successfully: **define** your "product through self-assessment; **analyze** your market by using your extensive network; **market** your product with well crafted resumes and cover letters; and **sell** your product during the interview process by translating your skills and assets into benefits for the employer. The final stage of the process is **evaluating** your options.

The day you accept a new job is the day you should be **the most** excited about that position. Accepting a job is a big deal. If you have any doubts, hesitations or reservations, stop and ask yourself if this is truly the job for you. Or, are you considering it out of desperation or fear that you will never find a suitable position? Consider whether you are simply trading one difficult situation for another.

If, however, you are genuinely excited about the possibilities the position presents, accept the position. It may be helpful to review Chapter 4 to determine how good a fit the position is for you.

Once you have accepted the position, send your new employer a thank you note expressing your enthusiasm for the job. This will reinforce in the employer's mind that the right candidate was selected.

Remember to inform all those who have been helpful to you along the way. Send letters to people about your new position, thank them for their assistance and support and offer to return the favor in the future.

13

ALTERNATIVES TO PRACTICING LAW

Given the dissatisfaction rampant in the legal profession and the problems inherent in creating a part-time schedule, many lawyers now face tremendously difficult decisions:

- Do I give up the practice of law entirely?
- Is there some way to combine my practice with my other, equally important interests?
- Can I combine my practice with raising a family?
- If I do give up my practice, what else can I do with a law degree?
- How much money will I earn?
- How do I find a new job?

These questions, which have become all too common, often lead to a state of panic from which no rational decision can be made. There are no Martindale-Hubbell listings for nontraditional or part-time lawyers. For lawyers trained in the highly structured law school environment where getting hired was almost part of the curriculum, the prospect of leaving the profession can be daunting.

The good news for the lawyer pursuing alternative work arrangements is that what first appears as a murky road toward instability can be broken down systematically and logically into a series of viable options. Even more encouraging is the tremendous wealth of resource materials that have appeared in recent years. The world of nontraditional/alternative careers has developed into a veritable industry, ranging from books to newsletters to specialized career counseling consultants. As the industry evolves, these positions will become both more readily available and more "acceptable" in the eyes of the legal profession.

In general, making the move out of a traditional legal position involves three components: self-assessment, analysis of possible options, and decision making implementation. Examination of these components should not be treated in a simplistic manner. If you are dissatisfied with your practice, think about exactly why you are unhappy. Do you really dislike the practice of law? Or is it just that you hate writing briefs? Or that you hate working until 9:00 p.m. most nights and can't juggle work and family? Or that you hate living in a large urban environment?

Since practice in the legal profession is preceded by a rigorous course of study most often extracting a three-year commitment of time, energy and financial resources, it is readily understandable that any lawyer would first give serious thought to the implications of making a major move. A comprehensive self-assessment to elicit the potential for change may include, among other things, one's tenure and progression in the legal profession, the skills and experience acquired that may be transferred to another setting, the compensation differentials that may accompany such a change, the substantive knowledge required, the impact on personal or family lifestyle, whether the change translates into short-term or long-term employment, and most important, whether making the change will bring success in achieving the lawyer's ultimate goal.

After careful thought and analysis many lawyers realize it is not the practice of law in itself that bothers them. For example, one lawyer realized he was unhappy because he hated writing the memos and briefs necessary to litigation. He is now happily employed as a corporate lawyer with a large biomedical engineering company. Some lawyers, of course, do realize they were never intended to be lawyers in the first place and choose to make a gracious exit. Coming to an understanding of why they do not enjoy practicing law allows them to be firm in the knowledge that they have exhausted their options and frees them of guilt and doubt about leaving the profession.

PROFILES OF LAWYERS WHO HAVE LEFT THE LAW

From Lawyer to Law-Related Position

David: Litigator to Bank Vice-President

David started his career as a standard litigator for a mid-sized firm in a large urban city. Like many other law graduates he had taken the best (and only) job that had been offered to him. Soon he wearied of the long hours, the long commute, and the adversarial nature of litigation. Two partners in the firm who practiced trusts and estates law asked him if he would like to work on a project, and he jumped at the chance.

Liking the calmer atmosphere and regular hours typical of trusts and estates work, David began to work exclusively for the two partners. He also started to work with trust officers in banks and got the idea that working in a bank would provide even more regular hours and a better quality of life. He used the annual listing of private banking departments in *Trusts and Estates* magazine, a trade publication his law firm received, as the basis for a mailing list.

Two months and twenty resumes later, he landed a job as a Trust Officer for one of the most prestigious banks in the country. Although he took a ten percent pay cut, the money was still quite good. As a Trust Officer, he works with the bank's wealthy clients on estates and trust accounts. The position is not in the legal department of the bank but does involve working with attorneys from outside firms.

David found the change from working in a law firm very refreshing. Everyone left at a reasonable hour in the evenings and weekend work was very rare. Family life outside of work was appreciated. The work itself was much less challenging, which was a mixed blessing. The pressure of law firm life had ebbed considerably, but David found himself doing a lot of paperwork that the paralegals would have ordinarily done in a law firm. There were also some glamorous aspects to the job, however, such as attending auctions at Sotheby's and Christie's for clients. "Like everything else in life, it was a trade off."

"Ironically, this type of job is perfect for outgoing, yet detail oriented people," according to David. The work itself is tremendously detail oriented and paper intensive. However, the position also requires an ability to entertain, win and retain clients and to bring in new accounts for the bank. In recent years the pressure to bring in business has increased as banks, like law firms, face increased economic hurdles.

After four years, David was promoted to Vice President. If he were to stay at the bank, he could pursue career paths in management or move laterally into a marketing oriented or financial (portfolio management) position. However, at this time David has mixed feelings about remaining in banking. "It is very corporate, very image oriented, and requires you to conform to certain modes of behavior and a very corporate culture", he said. Other possible related career paths he is considering would include working for a foundation or as a director of planned giving in a hospital or academic environment.

Moving to a Law Related Position: Emphasize Transferable Skills

Trust Officer:

Job Description:	Transferable Skills From Law:
Works with Documents	Document Drafting/Reviewing
Prepares Estate Tax Returns	Knowledge of the Tax Code
Manages Trust Accounts	Ability to Work with Numbers
Recommends Financial Options	Detail Oriented
Works with Wealthy Clients	Ability to Gain Confidence of Powerful Clients

---

From Full Time Lawyer to "Moonlighter"

Gail: Corporate Lawyer to Pasty Chef/Part-Time Lawyer

Some lawyers practice law on a full- or part-time basis and pursue an entirely different career "after hours." Some of these lawyers have come to terms with the fact that they do not enjoy practicing law but accept it as a means of financing what they really do enjoy.

The concept behind moonlighting is that many of these lawyers are happier with their lives overall even if they do not enjoy the "legal" half of their day. Generally their goal is eventually to move completely away from the law if their new career becomes sufficiently lucrative. At a recent panel discussion on this topic, a member of the audience asked how it was humanly possible to practice law and moonlight at night. A panelist who does both responded that the sheer enjoyment of her "moonlighting" as an artist was energizing rather than exhausting.

Indeed many lawyers recently have come to the same conclusions. One notable example is Scott Turow, author of *Presumed Innocent* and *Burden of Proof* and partner at Sonnenschein, Nath & Rosenthal, who writes during his daily train commute to work.

Gail, like David, took the best offer she got after interviewing on-campus at law school. She became a corporate attorney at a large law firm in the Midwest. At first, the job was very exciting. She was involved in high profile transactions and enjoyed the financial perks and comfortable lifestyle afforded by life in a large law firm.

After several years she started to become unhappy with the practice of law. "I'm capable at this, but I basically have no deepseated interest in finance or corporate law." Like many bright attorneys, she was doing well at her job but not moved by it.

Gail interviewed for a job in another area of the firm which did international corporate transactions. Again, she was interacting with high profile people, and traveled to Europe on business several times. Eventually, the same sense of dissatisfaction set in. She was still practicing corporate law, and becoming increasingly disinterested. At this point she had been working for the firm for seven years.

After considering (and rejecting) related positions, Gail finally decided to make the break. She gave notice and left her position with the law firm.

Gail then focused on what she liked to do outside of the practice of law, with the help of a career counselor. She had always been interested in writing, cooking and acting. She decided to enroll in a professional cooking school and started a year long course to become a pastry chef. She soon found herself happily immersed in the complexities of marzipan and butter cream frosting.

At the same time, as soon as she quit her job, new opportunities appeared. A former colleague and friend from the firm asked her to work part-time on several projects at a small private law firm. The theater group that she had been volunteering with asked her to cater one of their functions.

Like David, Gail has somewhat mixed feelings about her new life. She was very surprised, and gratified to find that leaving her job actually caused new, previously unanticipated opportunities to present themselves to her. She was amazed at the support (and sometimes envy) she received from her colleagues, her friends and her spouse.

However, she and her family have had to make some financial sacrifices and halfway through the year long course she has some doubts as to whether or not she wants to become a professional chef. Her feelings towards practicing law and giving up her high profile image are also unresolved. But she is more at peace with herself. "Towards the end of my career as a full-time lawyer I was unable to sleep." For now, Gail has decided to stick with cooking school. And the results may be sweet indeed. "The pastry course graduates have a one hundred percent employment rate." Gail may soon find many other lawyers joining her class.

Making the Break from Law Practice:
Pursue Your True Love Full-time and Turn Your Hobby
into a Full-Fledged Career

- Try to remember what you liked to do before you became a lawyer
- Do self assessment exercises to highlight your interests
- Do volunteer work, take courses, or moonlight first
- Work part-time as a lawyer while developing your interest into a business
- Convince yourself that it's okay to enjoy what you are doing

---

From Lawyer to Non-Legal Professional

Andrea: Government Lawyer to Journalist

One of the problems lawyers face in moving out of a traditional legal position is impatience. Yet slowing down can ultimately lead to a much more satisfying position. A move to a better quality of life with reduced work hours or a move to a nonlegal position may need to be accomplished through a two- or three-step transition. For example, a corporate lawyer at an urban law firm who found the work tedious and the hours incompatible with raising two children was able to make a successful two-step transition. She first took her corporate skills to an in-house position in a corporation in a suburban area. After establishing herself within the corporation and making friends with the right people, she was able to network herself into a nonlegal position doing corporate communications.

Once you are well liked within an organization, your employers will be more predisposed to accommodate you than if you were to approach them cold from the outside.

The day that Ronald Reagan was shot in the shoulder changed Andrea's life forever. Andrea, who graduated from a top ten law school in the late seventies, had taken a job in Washington, D.C. with a large government agency.

She was busy at work one day when she learned that Ronald Reagan had been shot outside of the Hilton Hotel. Curious, she walked from her nearby office to the hospital. Reporters, television crews, and police officers were excitedly trying to get information and control the crowds. At that moment, Andrea, observing the reporters at work, realized with sudden clarity that she was observing her own life dream: to be a journalist. She left the crime scene, and never went back to her office.

Soon after that day she sent away for applications to journalism school, and was shortly accepted by Columbia University's prestigious program. After working for several womens' magazines for a short time af ter graduating, she received an offer from a national newsmagazine to be a reporter. She has been working there ever since, covering legal issues and the Supreme Court for the magazine.

Andrea never looked back and never regretted her decision. "Life is too short," she said. Her chosen profession, like all others, is not without drawbacks. It involves hours that are comparable with practicing law, and is somewhat less lucrative. But Andrea knows in her heart that she is doing what she loves best. She had the courage to follow her instincts and is now at the top of her chosen profession.

Taking a Step Back to Move Forward
Going Back to School to Change Careers

Sometimes changing careers involves obtaining another advanced degree. Lawyers have most commonly enrolled in graduate programs in:

- Journalism (MA. In Journalism or Communications)
- Psychology (Ph.D.)
- Business (M.B.A.)

NONLEGAL AND LEGALLY RELATED JOB TITLES:

Although there is no magical "list" of jobs for lawyers (especially high paying jobs), the following job titles held by lawyers may serve as means for brainstorming. We either personally know or have heard about a lawyer transitioning into every job title listed.

Agent
Arbitrator
Assistant/Associate Dean
Auditor
Author
Accountant
Bank Vice President
Bar Association Administrator
Career Counselor
Certified Financial Planner
Commercial Real Estate Agent
Computer Consultant
Corporate Trainer
Contract Attorney
Department Store Buyer
Designer/Developer of Trial
   Visual Aides
Deposition Videographer
Director of Career Services,
   Admissions or Alumni Affairs
Editor
Executive Director of
   Nonprofit Agencies
Fundraiser

Investment Banker
Journalist
Jury Consultant
Law Librarian
Law Professor
Legislative Analyst
Lobbyist
Management Consultant
Mediator
Legal Software Developer/Vendor
Legal Consultant
Legal Headhunter
Politician/Political Advisor
President of a Corporation
Psychologist
Real Estate Developer
Restaurant Owner
Screenwriter
Small Business Owner
Special Event/Conference Planner
Stockbroker
Title Examiner
Trust Officer/Estate Administrator

As you begin to explore alternative career options, associations are an excellent place to start your research. Almost every industry has one or more associations analogous to the American Bar Association. Most associations can provide you with information, a calendar of events, a membership directory and committee roster, educational programming information and a newsletter, often containing job listings.

What follows is a comprehensive list of associations in industries in which lawyers are likely to transition.

ASSOCIATIONS FOR EXPLORING ALTERNATIVE CAREERS

FINANCIAL SERVICES

Accounts and Auditors

National Association Of Accountants
10 Paragon Drive
P. O. Box 433
Montvale, NJ 27645

National Society of Public Accountants
1010 North Fairfax Street
Alexandra, VA 22314

Institute of Internal Auditors
249 Maitland Avenue
Altamonte Springs, FL 32701

American Society of Women Accountants
35 East Wacker Drive
Chicago, IL 60601

American Institute of Certified Public Accountants
1211 Avenues of the Americans
New York, NY 10036-8775

Banking Administrators and Managers

American Bankers Association
Bank Personnel Division
1120 Connecticut Avenue, NW
Washington, DC 20036

Bank Administration Institute
60 Gould Center
Rolling Meadows, IL 60008

National Bankers Association
122 C Street, NW Suite 240
Washington, DC 20001

Budget Analysts

U. S. Office of Personnel Management
1900 E Street, NW
Washington, DC 20415

Financial Planners and Managers

College for Financial Planning
9725 East Hampden Avenue
Denver, CO 80231

International Board of Standards & Practices
for Certified Financial Planners, Inc. (IBCFP)
5445 DTC Parkway, Suite P-1
Englewood, CO 80111

Insurance Agents and Brokers

(LIFE INSURANCE AGENT OR BROKER)
Insurance Institute of America
Providence and Sugartown Roads
Malvern, PA 19355

(CASUALTY INSURANCE AGENT OR BROKER)
Insurance Information Institute
110 William Street
New York, NY 10038

Independent Insurance Agents of America
100 Church Street
New York, NY 10007

Professional Insurance Agents
400 North Washington Street
Alexandria, VA 22314

Investment Bankers

National Association of Securities Dealers
1735 K Street NW
Washington, DC 20006

Securities Industry Association
120 Broadway
New York, NY 10271

Loan Officers

American Bankers Association
Bank Personnel Division
1120 Connecticut Avenue, NW
Washington, DC 20036

National Bankers Association
122 C Street, NW Suite 240
Washington, DC 20001

Bank Administration Institute
60 Gould Center
Rolling Meadows, IL 60008

Management Consultants

Association of Management Consultants
500 North Michigan Avenue
Chicago, IL 60611

Association of Management Consulting Firms, Inc.
230 Park Avenue
New York, NY 10169

Institute of Management Consultants
19 West 44th Street
New York, NY 10036

Securities Analysts

Institute of Chartered Financial Analysts
P. O. Box 3668
Charlottesville, VA 22903

Financial Analysts Federation
1633 Broadway, 16th Floor
New York, NY 10019

Securities Sales Representatives (Stockbrokers)

Securities Industry Association
120 Broadway
New York, NY 10271

SALES AND MARKETING

Advertising Managers and Account Executives

American Association of Advertising Agencies
666 Third Avenue, 13th Floor
New York, NY 10017

American Advertising Federation
1400 K Street, NW
Suite 1000
Washington, DC 20005

Association of National Advertisers
155 East 44th Street
New York, NY 10017

American Marketing Association
230 North Michigan Avenue
Chicago, IL 60606

Media Planners

American Advertising Federation
1400 K Street, NW Suite 1000
Washington, DC 20005

American Association of Advertising Agencies
666 Third Avenue
13th Floor
New York, NY 10017

Public Relations Specialist

For job opportunities in public relations send $1 to:
Service Department
Public Relations News
127 East 80th Street
New York, NY 10021

Purchasing Agents and Managers

National Association of Purchasing Management, Inc.
2055 East Centennial Circle
P. O. Box 22160
Tempe, AZ 85282

Real Estate Agents and Managers

American Society of Real Estate Counselors
430 North Michigan Avenue
Chicago, IL 60611

National Association of Realtors
430 North Michigan Avenue
Chicago, IL 60611

The National Association of Real Estate Brokers
5501 Eighth Street NW Suite 202
Washington, DC 20011

National Institute of Realtors
Department of Education
155 East Superior Street
Chicago, IL 60611

Sales and Marketing Executives

American Marketing Association
250 South Wacker Drive Suite 200
Chicago, IL 60606-5819

Sales and Marketing Executives, International
446 Statler Office Tower
Cleveland, OH 44115

Wholesale and Retail Buyers

National Retail Merchants Association
100 West 31st Street
New York, NY 10001

ARCHITECTURE/ENGINEERING/COMPUTER SCIENCE

Chief Information Officers

Association for Systems Management
24587 Bagley Road
Cleveland, OH 44138

Civil Engineers

American Society of Civil Engineers
345 East 47th Street
New York, NY 10017

Computer Programers

Data Processing Management Association
505 Busse Highway
Park Ridge, IL 60068

Association of Computer Programmers & Analysts
2108-C Gallows Road
Vienna, VA 22180

IEEE (Institute of Electrical and Electronics
Engineers) Computer Society
1730 Massachusetts Ave., NW
Washington, DC 20036

Microcomputer Software Association
1300 North 17th Street, No. 300
Arlington, VA 22209

Association for Computing Machinery, Special
    Interest Group on Programming Languages
11 West 42nd Street, Third Floor
New York, NY 10036

Computer Security Specialists

Information Systems Security Association
P.O. Box 9457
Newport Beach, CA 92658

Computer Systems Analysts

Association for Systems Management
24587 Bagley Road
Cleveland, OH 44138

NATURAL SCIENCE AND MATHEMATICS

Mathematicians

American Mathematical Society
P. O. Box 6348
Providence, RI 02940

Mathematical Association of America
1529 18th Street, NW
Washington, DC 20036

Society for Industrial and Applied Mathematics
1400 Architects Building
117 South 17th Street
Philadelphia, PA 19103

Institute of Mathematical Statistics
3401 Investment Boulevard, No. 7
Hayward, CA 94545

Science Technicians

American Chemical Society
Career Services
1155 16th Street, NW
Washington, DC 20036

Naomi Williams, President
National Conference of Chemical Technician
Affiliates of the American Chemical Society
Monsato Co., Q3D
800 North Lindbergh Boulevard
St. Louis, MO 63167

American Institute of Biological Sciences
730 11th Street, NW
Washington, DC 20001

SOCIAL SCIENCES, THE LAW, AND LAW ENFORCEMENT

Alcohol and Drug Counselors

National Clearinghouse on Alcoholism & Drug Abuse
    Information (NCADI)
P. O. Box 2345
Rockville, MD 20852

Alcohol and Drug Problems Association (ADPA)
444 North Capitol Street, NW Suite 181
Washington, DC 20001

National Association of Alcoholism & Drug Abuse Counselors
(NAADAC)
3717 Columbia Pike Suite 300
Arlington, VA 22204

National Association of Substance Abuse Trainers and Educators
(NAST)
Southern University of New Orleans Training Program
for the Control of Substance Abuse
6400 Press Drive
New Orleans, LA 70126

Corporate Trainers

American Society for Training and Development
600 Maryland Avenue, SW Suite 305
Washington, DC 20025

National Training Laboratory
P. O. Box 9155
Rosslyn Station
Arlington, VA 22209

Economists

America Economic Association
1313 21st Avenue South
Nashville, TN 37212-2786

Joint Council on Economic Education
432 Park Avenue South
New York, NY 10016

National Association of Business Economics
28349 Chagrin Boulevard Suite 203
Cleveland, OH 44122

Urban and Regional Planners

American Planning Association
1776 Massachusetts Avenue, NW
Washington, DC 20036

Association of Collegiate Schools of Planning
College of Design, Architecture, Art & Planning
University of Cincinnati
Cincinnati, OH 45221

National Planning Association
1616 P Street, NW Suite 400
Washington, DC 20036

EDUCATION AND LIBRARY SCIENCE

Adult and Vocational Educational Teachers

American Association for Adult and Continuing Education
1112 16th Street, NW Suite 420
Washington, DC 20036

American Vocational Association
1410 King Street
Alexandria, VA 22314

Archivists and Curators

Society of Americans Archivists
600 South Federal Street
Suite 504
Chicago, IL 60605

American Association of Museums
1225 I Street, NW Suite 200
Washington, DC 20005

Association of Art Museum Directors
41 East 65th Street
New York, NY 10021

American Association of Botanical Gardens
    and Arboreta
P. O. Box 206
Swarthmore, PA 19081

American Institute for Conservation of Historic
   and Artistic Works
3545 Williamsburg Lane, NW
Washington, DC 20008

ADDITIONAL RESOURCES

Encyclopedia of Associations
Gale Research, Inc.
P.O. Box 33477
Detroit, MI 48323-5477
313-962-2242

Encyclopedia of Business Information
Gale Research, Inc.
P.O. Box 33477
Detroit, MI 48323-5477
313-962-2242

Directory of On-Line Databases
Gale Research, Inc.
P.O. Box 33477
Detroit, MI 48323-5477
312-962-2242

National Executive Search Corps
275 Park Avenue S
New York, NY 10010
212-529-6660

International Executive Service Corps
P.O. Box 1005
Stamford, CT 06904
203-967-6000

Executive Recruiter News ($15.00)
Templeton Road
Fitzwilliam, NH 03447
800-531-0007

Directory of Trade Shows
312-579-9090

Association Meeting Directory
800-541-0663

Directory of Consulting Organizations
313-962-2242

ELECTRONIC JOB SEARCH RESOURCES

For a fee ranging from $25 to $90, job seekers can have their professional credentials, experiences and background entered into a database of available talent and classified by certain criteria including position sought, industry, educational background, salary expectations, geographical preferences, special skills and other characteristics. Employers seeking to fill positions pay a fee to search for candidates whose qualifications match their requirements. For more information, refer to *Electronic Job Search Revolution*, by Joyce Lain Kennedy and Thomas J. Morrow.

Career Database
104 Mt. Auburn Street, 5th Floor
P.O. Box 2341, Cambridge, MA 02238
Telephone: (617) 876-9521; Fax: (617) 661-1575
   Used by companies and recruiters of all sizes, from Fortune 500 corporations to startup firms, and large search firms to small, specialized recruiters.

Career Placement Registry
Career Placement Registry Inc.,
302 Swann Avenue, Alexandria, VA 22301
Telephone: (800) 368-3093 or (703) 683-1085; Fax: (703) 683-0246
   Fortune 1000 companies, insurance companies, banks, industrial companies, government agencies, and nonprofit organizations access the database. Some 1,500 companies and organizations are CPR clients.

Job Bank USA
1420 Spring Hill Road, Suite 480
McLean, VA 22102
Telephone: (800) 296-1USA; Fax; (703) 847-1494
  350 active client employers, ranging in size from major international
  corporations and Fortune 500 firms to regional and local employers.

National Resume Bank
3637 4th Street North, No.330
St. Petersburg, FL 33704
Telephone: (813) 896-3694; Fax: (813) 894-1277
  Aerospace, Airlines, Casino (gambling), Clerical, Communications,
  Creative, Data Processing, Education, Engineering/Technical,
  Entertainment, Financial, Government/Public Service, Health Care,
  Hospitality, Legal, Management, Manufacturing, Real Estate, Retail,
  Sales, Trades

SkillSearch
104 Woodmont Boulevard, Suite 306
Nashville, TN 37025
Telephone: (800) 252-5665; Fax (615) 383-4743
  Fortune 1000 corporations, nonprofit organizations, and govern-
  mental agencies, as well as small to medium size companies.

SALARIES FOR ALTERNATIVE LEGAL CAREERS

When most people come in to inquire about nonlegal career options,
salaries are their primary concern. "What can I do where I will make as
much money as I am now, but not have to practice law?" they ask,
hopefully.

Not very much, unfortunately. Lawyers are among the most highly
salaried professionals in the "food chain." However, many attorneys have
no idea how much other professions pay. It is possible to earn a very
satisfactory living in other professions. Often a much more reasonable
lifestyle is a viable tradeoff for lost earnings. And as we saw in Andrea's
profile, doing what you love most is often what you have the most talent
for—and pays off in the long run.

CONCLUSION

The path to a nontraditional legal position is challenging. As you explore your options, keep in mind the following:

- **Always trust your own instincts.** Do not be scared off by peer pressure or anyone else's advice. Even if you are not sure where your instincts will lead you will almost always be headed in the right direction. You should feel no embarrassment in not being a 12-hour-a-day lawyer, nor should you feel any guilt associated with not being a lawyer at all. There is no reason to be trapped forever by a decision made at the age of 21.

- **Try not to let money completely rule your life.** Granted, almost everyone has financial obligations. Money is an extremely important factor in most career decisions. However, a substantial number of legal, law-related, and nonlegal positions pay very acceptable salaries. Before seeking a new position, write out a detailed budget for yourself and your family.

- **Motivate yourself.** It is somewhat paradoxical that lawyers, who are often highly motivated and adept at massive research, are so resistant to the legwork involved in a job search. Remember, as you have already learned the majority of jobs are never advertised. They are discovered through networking, personal contacts, and research rather than through recruiters or published ads. Call on friends, colleagues, and professionals such as your undergraduate or law school's career services staff for support and motivation. In this way you can assure yourself that you have explored, in depth, options for a career change or alternative work arrangements.

JOB AND EMPLOYER DESCRIPTIONS SURVEY

The diversity of jobs and employer types for professionals with J.D. degrees is illustrated by the graduating Class of 1994. Below is a representative sample of descriptions reported by the National Association for Law Placement's Class of 1994 Employment Report and Salary Survey for jobs of all types **outside** the realm of attorney in private practice or in the government in a prosecution, defender or military capacity for members of that class.

American Association of
  Retired Persons
Academic Research
Academic Advising
ACLU
Actress
ADA Consultant
Administrative Law for Utilities
Administrator - Juvenile Justice
  Program
Admissions Recruiting
  Director
Aerospace Engineer
AFL-CIO
AFSCME
Agency for International
  Development
Air Traffic Control Specialist
Airline
American Petroleum Institute
AMTRAK
Amusement Park Business
Appraiser
Architect
Architectural Engineer
Army Research
Assistant Vice President of
  Student Affairs
Assistant Commonwealth Attorney
Assistant Chief of Police
Assistant Project Director
Assistant Professor
Associate Editor
Association of Towns
Association of Security Dealers
Asylum Officer

Attorney in US Trustee Office
Attorney for Florida Senate
Auto Salvage
Bailiff
Bank Trust Department
Bankers' Association
Bankruptcy Specialist
Bar Association
Bar/Bri Representative
Bartender
Basketball Coach
Benefits Consulting
Bio-Medical Research
Biotech Consultant
Broadcasting
Brokerage Firm
Building Homes
Bureau of Indian Affairs
Bureau of Land Management
Cancer Research
Capitol Hill
Case Worker
Catering
Ceramics Production
Chancery Court
Chemist
Child Care
Child Support Enforcement
  Agency
Children's Court
Children's Protective Services
Chiropractor
Chamber of Commerce
Church Youth Leader
City Council
City Attorney's Office

City Solicitor's Office
City Council - Chief Aide
Civil Engineer - Project Manager
Civil Rights Litigation
Civil Litigation
Claims Representative
Claims Adjustor
Clerks of Courts
Cleveland Tenants' Organization
Commissioner of College
  Athletics
Communications Director
Compliance Officer
Computer Analyst
Computer Systems Consultant
Congressional Staff
Congressional Campaign
Congresswoman
Consulate/Japan
Consultant for National Health
  Care Group
Contract Administration
Copper Mining Corporation
Corporate Manager
Corporate Senior Credit Officer
Corporation Counsel
Counsel for Indian Tribe
Counsel NYC Housing Authority
County Probate Court
Court Administration
Court Liaison - Social Worker
Court TV
CPA
Crafts
Criminal Appeals
Customer Service
Dean of Community College
Department of Corrections
Department of Environmental
  Protection
Department of Buildings

Department of Housing
  Preservation
Department of Education
Department of Interior
Department of Revenue
Department of Highways
Department Store
DePaul Human Rights Institute
Director of Legal Research
Director of Library
Director of Financial Aid
Disposal Service
DOD Research Analyst
Editor/Humanitarian
Editor
Electric and Gas Utility
Electronics Engineering Firm
Elementary School Teacher
Employment Commission -
  Tribunal
Engineer
Engineering Contracts Manager
Entertainment Industry Executive
Environmental Consultant
Environmental Defense Fund
Environment Law Reporter
EPA
Executive Assistant
Executive Director of Community
  Center
Executive Director of Mental
  Health Board
Family Business
Family Law Center
Family Restaurant Business
Farmworker Advocacy
FBI
FDIC
Federal Reserve Bank
Federal Elections Commission
Film Industry

Financial Analyst
Financial Services
Firefighter
Food Business
Forensic Chemist
Free Lance Translator
Fund Manager
General Manager
General Service Administration
Governor's Office
Governor's Transition Team
Grant Manager
Hat Shop
Health Care Risk Management
Health Care
Hearings Examiner
High School Business Law
  Teacher
High School Teacher
Horse Trainer
Hospital Administrator
Housing Inspector
Housing Authority
Human Resources Consulting
  Firm
IL Supreme Court Research
  Department
Income Tax Preparation
Instructor at FBI Academy
Insurance Agent
International Life Sciences
  Institute
International Trade Commission
International Red Cross
Investigative Services
Investment Banker
Irish American Cultural Institute
IRS Attorney
IRS Taxpayer Service
  Representative
Journalism

Juvenile Court
Juvenile Counselor
Labor Union
Law School Admissions
League of Minnesota Cities
Legal Publishing
Legal Director
Legal Secretary
Legislative Analyst
Legislative Aide
Librarian
Lighting Consultant
Linguist
Lithuanian Commercial Company
Litigation Support
Litigation Graphics Consultant
Lobbyist
Major Talent Agency
Management Consulting
Manager - Environmental and
  Regulatory Affairs
Marketing
Marketing for International Lottery
and Gaming Corporation
Mechanical Engineer
Mediator for County
Medical Technician
Merit Systems Protection Board
Minister
Mortgage Loan Processing
Municipal Attorney
Municipal League
Museum Security
NAPIL
NASA
National Public Radio
National Association of Attorneys
  General
National Labor Relations Board
Native Americans in DC
New Zealand Parliament

NFL
Nurse
NYC Transit Authority
NYC Corporation Counsel
Occupational Safety and Health
  Administration
Office of U.S Trade
  Representative
Office of Personnel Management
Oil and Gas Corporation
Oklahoma Housing Finance
  Agency
Olympic committee
Paralegal
Parks Department
Parole Officer
Pasta Manufacturer and Restaurant
Peace Corps
Pediatrician
Pharmaceutical Company
Pharmacist
Physical Therapist
Pilot
Police Officer
Policy Analyst
Political Consultant
Polymer Research
Portrait Studio
Pre-Hearing Attorney
Pre-Trial Service
Press Secretary
Probation Officer
Procurement Attorney
Professional Sports Manager
Professional Basketball
Program Director
Project Coordinator for NYPIRG
Psychometrist - Special Ed
Public Health Service
Publishing
Purchasing

Radiation Research
Railroad Authority
Real Estate Investment and
  Management
Real Estate Development
Realtor
Record Company
Recruiter for Law School
Referee
Regulatory Agency
Research Assistant
Resolution Trust Corporation
Restaurant
Retail
Retired Teacher's Association
Rock Band Manager
Sales
School Board
School for Blind
Secretary of State's Office
Securities and Exchange
  Commission
Securities - Marketing and
  Compliance
Self-Employed
Senate Committee Counsel
Senatorial Aide
Senior Economist
Sewer District
Shareholder Compliance
Sierra Club
Small Business Administration
Social Security Administration
Social Worker
Software Consulting
Special Agent - U.S. Customs
Sports Public Relations
Sports Management
Staff Attorney - State Gambling
  Commission
State Public Utility Regulation

State Detention Officer
Stock Broker
Store Detective
Systems Analyst
Tax Examiner
Teacher of English to Foreign
  Students
Teaching at Prep School
Teaching Paralegals at Business
  School
Teamsters Local 205
Tenant Resource Center
Territorial Government
Timber Council

Tire Wholesaler
Title Company
Title Examiner
Tribal Attorney
U.S. Marshall's Service
U.S. Patent and Trademark Office
UNICEF - Assistant Project
  Officer
United Mine Workers
Venture Capital Group
Vice-President
Wastewater Treatment Facility
Writer

14

STRATEGIES FOR SURVIVING UNEMPLOYMENT

A sudden layoff in today's job market may not be surprising but can still be devastating both financially and emotionally. There are many highly qualified people who are unemployed through no fault of their own. Recouping your self-esteem is the hardest part of the job search process, since losing a job is an emotional separation from which it is natural to grieve. Similarly, recent graduates who have survived three years of law school only to discover that there is no job waiting for them also can be devastated emotionally and financially. Although both groups need time to process feelings, the best way to recover is to take action. Creating a plan of action, starting your job search, establishing goals and brainstorming with others will restore your energy and make you think about the future instead of brood about the past. Consider the following strategies to help you speed up your recovery time.

- **Negotiate your severance agreement.** Realize that despite everything, you still have some bargaining power even as you are walking out the door. Your former employer would like to remain on good terms with you and see that you leave with a minimum of hostility. Ask for anything that would be helpful to you. At this point, you have nothing to lose. You may be able to negotiate severance pay, continued use of an office or other space, secretarial privileges (including answering service). You should clarify the employer's position on these issues before you actually leave. Recent graduates should contact lending institutions to inquire about loan deferments.

- **Request Outplacement Services.** Many employers retain outplacement companies as a goodwill gesture to help displaced employees get started with their job search. These companies provide career counseling as well as instructions in networking, resume writing, cover letter drafting, interviewing and follow-up techniques. Take advantage of these services but be mindful to adapt their suggestions to your particular needs.

- **Request References.** You should have a conversation with the person or persons who will act as your references and come to a mutual agreement as to what will be said. You can initiate this conversation and actually tell them, to some extent, what you would like them to say. They are likely to agree with any reasonable suggestion. Although most employers desire phone references, you may also want to ask for a written letter of reference to use as a back up. Again, it is vitally important to actually have the letter in hand when you leave. References are equally important for new graduates. Faculty members and former employers should be approached for ref-erences and referrals.

- **Apply for Unemployment and Health Benefits.** Unless you were fired "for cause," you are usually entitled to unemployment benefits although severance payment that you collect may affect the amount of unemployment benefits you receive. You should register for unemployment right away, as it may take some time to receive it. The good news is that you can receive every check except for the first one mailed to you at home from some employment offices. You will not necessarily lose your health insurance coverage either. You are entitled by law in most cases to extend your health benefits (although you have to make the monthly payments) for up to eighteen months under COBRA, the Consolidated Omnibus Budget Reconciliation Act. You may also want to consider joining professional associations that offer group health coverage to members.

Viewing a termination as a positive experience sounds like a contradiction in terms. After all, termination is basically a rejection. People have described the trauma of feeling like a victim. Being associated with a particular firm or organization can be such an important part of a person's life. Being laid off not only creates a tremendous sense of loss of structure and interruption of "normal" daily routines but also a sense of betrayal. The firm or organization loses its family, caring atmosphere as the blame gets spread around and becomes anonymous, with nobody taking responsibility. The financial blow and the change in consumer status can be equally devastating.

In social situations, we are always defined by what we do for a living. Being laid off makes for some awkward moments when meeting new people. Rather than avoid much needed social engagements (and networking opportunities!) consider how you will respond when met with the question "What do you do?" Obviously, it is still appropriate to say, "I am an attorney, and you?" If pressed for more information, ("Really, who are you with?") try turning an awkward moment into a networking opportunity by simply saying "I am in transition at the moment. My background is in ...."

In Chinese, the symbol for crisis is the same as the symbol for opportunity. A layoff isn't only a crisis, but also a unique opportunity. It forces you to really look at your values and priorities and provides a push to change things for the better.

During a challenging search, your emotional well-being deserves attention and care. In fact, your productivity and ultimate success depend on it. Monitor your feelings and, when necessary, take aggressive, vigorous action to shift them in a positive direction. Since people need to feel they are making some progress in order to keep pursuing their goals, job hunters faced with frequent setbacks and disappointments may eventually lose all hope of finding a suitable position. Typically the "job market" treats candidates with little consideration or care. The trauma of the downsizing followed by a protracted search may paralyze you with depression, anxiety, frustration and anger. When you are feeling overwhelmingly discouraged, consider these tips to help you recharge emotionally and get over the "Why bother?" hump.

1. **Analyze the panic—what is the fear?**

   "I will never work again."
   "I won't get the job I want."
   "I won't get the salary I want."

   How real are these fears? How can you prepare for, minimize or render any of these scenarios temporary?

2. **Focus on what you can control.** Understand that each stage of the hiring cycle has lengthened. There is little you can do to speed up the process. You can not make employers waive requirements, create openings or return your calls. The more you try to plan or control these factors, the harder and more frustrating your search will be. Fuming over the fact that companies rarely confirm receipt of your resume or that they run blind ads is wasted energy. Focus on what you can control: the quality of your cover letters, resume, image, interviews, follow-up and networking. You can determine how fast you respond to leads, ideas and events. Concentrate your energies in these areas and let go of the rest.

3. **Take a career development refresher course.** Now you have personal experiences to relate to the theories. This could give your morale a boost.

4. **Share your anxieties with supportive friends/family.** Not only are these people great sounding boards but they can also help you spot flaws in your search. Remember to **ask for what you need**! Well meaning spouses and parents can drive a job seeker crazy by trying to be helpful or asking too many questions or by just plain nagging. Enlist their help as a coach if you think it would be productive. Otherwise, politely ask them to leave you alone while you sort through things.

   Keep in mind a change in your life naturally means a change in the life of your family members. They may be scared or have questions too. Do not try to protect loved ones by acting in control. They will be more supportive if they know what is going on and understand how they can be helpful.

5. **Try professional counseling.** An experienced counselor can provide focus, guidance, motivation, evaluation, market knowledge and coaching. Don't forget to take advantage of the services of your law school's career services office.

6. **Have some fun.** Do not feel guilty about enjoying something or goofing off periodically. Exercise, take a short trip to refresh yourself, tackle a project or read a novel. A short time away from your job search may allow you to return with renewed vigor and energy.

Although no one would have wished for a recession in the legal field, many have benefited from it by being forced to give some serious thought to their careers. Even those who remain unemployed for extended periods can be rejuvenated by the experience. By taking some time to reassess yourself, you can change your life and hopefully move in a new and better direction. Many people end up happier after a transition.

15

ANSWERS TO THE 15 MOST COMMONLY ASKED QUESTIONS

1. Question: I have been asked what my salary requirements are. How can I answer the question without blowing my chances?

     Answer: Salary questions are tough, but manageable. If you can, get the employer to state a figure first. If not, try to give a ten thousand dollar range, instead of naming a specific figure. Think about a bottom line number that you can comfortably live with and bear that in mind during negotiating. Go for what you want, but also be willing to give something up; less money for better benefits, etc. Consult the *American Lawyer* annual law firm survey or *David J. White and Associates, Inc. Annual Salary Survey* for information about the going market rate.

2. Question: I can't network because I don't already have contacts. What should I do?

Answer: Everyone has contacts. Start close to home with family members, relatives, neighbors, coworkers, friends. Offer to take people for coffee, or for lunch. Have **face to face meetings** instead of phone conversations if possible. Just ask for advice and information, **not** a job. At the end of each meeting, ask if the person you are meeting with knows anyone else you can "brainstorm" with, for advice and information. Your network will start to expand as you are referred to people, like a spider web.

According to **Webster's New Collegiate Dictionary**, a network is " a fabric or structure of cords or wires that cross at regular intervals and are knotted or secured at the crossings." **You** will become the crossings, or center of this network as you continue to meet friends of friends.

3. Question: How can I switch to a different practice area when I don't have any work experience in that area?

Answer: In order to switch to a different practice area, you need to develop some knowledge of the area and be able to convince employers of your genuine interest in changing career direction. One way to accomplish this is to take continuing legal education courses, seminars, or workshops in your area of interest and add them to your resume under "Additional Training/Coursework." Another good idea is to join the committee of your state or local bar association in the area into which you

want to switch. Attend the meetings, get to know
the members, and **offer** to take charge of a
project. That way you will get to know people
and impress them with your willingness to learn
and to work hard. Pro Bono work in your
targeted area of practice is yet another way to
demonstrate interest in and gain knowledge of a
particular practice area.

4. Question: What are the alternative legal careers that most
lawyers go into?

Answer: There is no "magic list" of employers who like to
hire law school graduates. However, many, many
lawyers have transitioned into other fields. Entre-
preneurial ventures and the communications and
financial arenas have attracted many former
lawyers, but lawyers have gone into almost every
field imaginable. The place to start, as always, is
not with "what's available" but with yourself, by
doing in-depth self assessment. From that stand-
point you can then identify specific jobs, and
transferable skills. Although employers in other
fields often question why anyone would want to
leave law practice, they are usually impressed
with legal credentials.

5. Question: I did not get good grades in law school—who is
going to hire me?

Answer: Other than the top 10-15% of every law school,
every law school graduate experiences concern at
some time about their G.P.A. The good news is,
other than very large law firms, legal employers
are more concerned with your experience, your
ability to think and talk on your feet, your
analytical and writing skills, and **most of all** your
desire and enthusiasm for the position. Focusing
on a specific area or type of practice and gaining
a lot of experience in that area (paid or pro bono)
can compensate for less than stellar grades. If a

large law firm is your heart's desire, remember
that there are "many roads to mecca." Becoming
an expert in an area of practice that they want to
expand, or transitioning laterally after a few years
of practice can get you through the door.

6. Question: I have a job interview tomorrow—how can I find
out more about the law firm/agency/organ-
ization?

Answer: Consult your law school career services office to
see if they have any information about the
employer on file, and the alumni office to see if
there are any alumni already working there;
Research on-line services (Lexis and Westlaw)
both in the legal directories (NALP-DIR,
MARHUB, etc.), and in the news databases
(Nexis/Dialog/Dow Jones) for information. The
legal organizations on-line have increased on an
almost daily basis in recent years. Call the human
resources/recruitment department of the organization and ask if they have an annual report or
brochure about the organization. Go pick it up in
person from the department.

7. Question: There is a period of a year after law school/
between jobs when I didn't work. What should I
put on my resume? What if I get asked questions
about my employment history?

Answer: Gaps in employment are common, especially in
today's challenging economic times. If you have
done any pro bono work, per diem work or
continuing legal education, list it on your resume.
It is usually better to list your dates of employment on your resume on the right hand side of
your resume rather than the left margin. Since the
eye reads from left to right employers will be
focused on your employment experience, not the
length of time that you have worked. Prepare in
advance and practice how you will answer the

question in an interview situation. Remember to look the interviewer straight in the eye, lean forward slightly and smile. This will disarm the interviewer, because he will see that you are not flustered. Answer the question honestly, putting it in its most positive light. After you have answered the question, move on to another topic of conversation.

8. Question: I had a job interview with several attorneys and the recruitment coordinator—to whom should I send the thank you letter?

Answer: You should send the thank you letter to either the most senior level person, the recruitment co-ordinator, or to the person with whom you really "clicked" during the interview. You may send just one letter, but you must include a line in which you ask the interviewer to extend your thanks to all of the others who interviewed you (list them by name—make sure all names are spelled correctly). If you send individual letters, they must all be **different**. Mail your thank you letter as soon as possible after the interview.

9. Question: I just found out I'm getting laid off. What if anything should I ask the firm to do for me?

Answer: Arrange for a face to face meeting with your employer before you actually leave the job. Have the meeting after you have had a day or two to calm down and organize your thoughts. Write everything down that you would like to request before the meeting. You should ask about sev-erance pay, unemployment, outplacement/ career counseling services, references, use of a secretary or office space, and what both you and the employer will say to the outside world about the reason for your departure. Get everything nailed down before you actually leave. Once you have left, your former employer may be harder to reach and less motivated to respond quickly. Remember that you have some negotiating ability; both sides would prefer a peaceful resolution. Play to their "guilt" by asking for what you need. Most employers feel bad when they have to let an employee go and would be happy to have the opportunity to help.

10. Question: I can't fit everything onto one page of my resume—What should I take out?

Answer: If you cannot fit everything onto one page, try one or more the following suggestions: use the "bullet" format incorporating your sentences into short phrases preceded by a dot, dash or asterisk; eliminate job descriptions for positions which you held over ten years ago or which are not relevant to the job for which you are applying; create more than one version of your resume so that you can focus on different areas of experience for different positions; reduce the size of the font to ten or eleven point, or use a different font. If you do have a two page resume, make sure that your name, address and phone number appear at the top of the second page and that the second page is at least half full. The entire resume should be uncluttered and very easy to read. Place information that the potential employer must know on the first page.

11. Question: I went to a bar association function to try to meet people and network but I didn't know anyone there. How can I make contacts at events?

Answer: First of all, GO! Don't make excuses and stay at home. Bring a friend if you want to for moral support, but don't stay together once you have arrived. Promise yourself that you can leave after twenty minutes if you are not having a good time. Once there, position yourself between the entrance and the food/ bar where people can see you and you will always be surrounded by other people. When the event is in full swing, **circulate**, and make sure to bring business cards—you don't want to have to go through your purse/ pockets looking for a pencil in the middle of an important conversation.

12. Question: How many jobseekers actually get their jobs through some form of networking?

Answer: According to a report in *Forbes* magazine by a Harvard sociologist, "informal contacts" account for approximately seventy-five percent of all new jobs. Agencies/ headhunters find jobs for about ten percent and classified ads provide about ten percent.

13. Question: I got a job offer from a law firm, but I'm waiting to hear from another firm that I really would rather work for—what should I do?

Answer: This is a very common situation—you wait seemingly forever to get a job offer, and then you have to make a tough choice very suddenly. However, handled diplomatically you can usually buy yourself some time. When you call the firm back after having received the offer, show a lot of enthusiasm and appreciation, and thank them for the offer. You can then simply ask, "When do you need to know?" Most firms will give you approximately two weeks to consider the offer. Only very rarely will a firm withdraw your offer (and you would not want to work for them anyway). You should then let the other firm—the one you really want—know they need to make a decision about your application. Often having another offer makes you appear more desirable to them, and can work in your favor. If all things appear to be equal, trust your gut instinct.

14. Question: What are the "hot" legal practice areas right now?

Answer: Environmental law, international law, employment law and intellectual property are some of the popular specialty areas right now. However, the legal job market is very volatile and will probably continue to change in the next few years. The key to getting into a hot area is to predict it in advance, by carefully watching proposed government legislation and economic reforms. Track upcoming trends by getting into the habit of reading legal and nonlegal periodicals on a daily basis.

15. Question: What is **the most effective** technique for finding a job as a lawyer in today's marketplace?

Answer: You have to use a combination of job search techniques, and continue them on a regular basis. Doing your job search in stop and start spurts, or utilizing only one method such as answering classified ads is not the most successful approach. Doing a job search is like starting an exercise plan or a diet: you need to do a variety of exercises to get your whole body in shape, and eat several different types of foods to achieve a balanced diet. Just lifting weights or eating only broccoli may be good for you but it won't achieve your goals.

Conduct your job search through a combination of: networking, answering classified ads, researching organizations, attending events, sending out narrowly targeted mailings, and using headhunters/agencies. Continue on a steady basis until you land the job of your dreams. Don't give up until you find it.

Appendix A

SAMPLE
RESUMES

In addition to the resume writing information provided in Chapter Ten, we have assembled a variety of sample resumes. Included are examples of recent law graduates, junior, midlevel and senior level attorneys in different practice areas and settings as well as an example of a public interest/public service resume, and an "alternative legal career" resume.

The intent of these samples is to help get your creative juices flowing by illustrating the various content, style, and formats other job seekers have found effective. Please remember that there is no one right way to write a resume; above all, it must be your own, and you must be comfortable with it.

BAR STATUS

Passed New York State Bar; awaiting admission.

EDUCATION

Fordham University School of Law, New York, NY
J.D. May 1995; Cumulative GPA: 3.2; Third Year GPA: 3.6; Dean's List
  Third Year
Associate Editor, *Fordham Intellectual Property, Media & Entertainment
  Law Journal*
Co-Director, Fordham Law Community Service Project
Director, Fordham Law Habitat for Humanity
The Edmund Hennelly (Public Service) Scholarship
The Archibald R. Murray Public Service Award

New York University, New York, NY
M.S. in Commercial Real Estate, 1992; GPA: 3.6

The College of the Holy Cross, Worcester, MA
B.A., Double majors in History and French, 1987; GPA: 3.25
Dean's List - Three semesters; Pierre Bourgeois Prize for Essay on French
  Culture

EXPERIENCE

Townsend & Valente, New York, NY, *Research Assistant* - Spring 1995
Researched state tax law for pending case before the New York State Tax
Appeals Tribunal.

Hon. John L. Caden, United States Magistrate Judge, E.D.N.Y., *Student
Law Clerk* - Fall 1994
Drafted decisions for *habeas corpus* petition and insurance fraud case.
Observed federal court proceedings.

Skadden, Arps, Slate, Meagher & Flom, New York, NY, *Pro Bono
Research Assistant* - Fall 1994
Conducted extensive research and writing for capital punishment appellate
review.

Cassin, Cassin & Joseph, New York, NY, *Legal Assistant* - June 1993 -
September 1994
Prepared real estate and co-op closing documents, including mortgages,
notes, settlement statements, proprietary leases, and title and lien searches.
Closed over 300 transactions on behalf of 12 client banks.

Hon. Manuel Del Valle, New York State Division of Human Rights, New York, NY, *Law Clerk* - Spring 1994
Drafted proposed decision in disability discrimination case for Division's Chief Administrative Law Judge.

New York City Loft Board, New York, NY, *Summer Law Clerk* - Summer 1993
Researched procedural, substantive and administrative law; drafted opinion In Re 334 Bowery, 15 L.B.R. -- (1993).

Banque Nationale de Paris, New York, NY, *Account Administrator* - 1989 - 1992
Provided construction loans and refinancing for commercial real estate. Assisted in administration and disposal of problem properties. Versed in commercial investment and lending instruments and bank accounting procedures.

Internal Revenue Service, Cleveland, OH, *Tax Research Assistant* - 1987-1988
Researched federal tax code to assist small business and individual filers with various federal taxes.

LANGUAGES

Fluent in French, studies in German and Spanish.

NAME
Address
Phone

LEGAL EMPLOYMENT:

BATTLE FOWLER   New York, New York
Associate, Real Estate Department   *August 1993 - Present*
Reviewed title and drafted loan documents and supporting collateral agreements in connection with eight commercial loans ($10 million to $200 million) by two major insurance companies. Drafted transfer documents for lender in two bulk sale transactions of commercial properties (hotels, apartment houses and office buildings) located in eight states. Drafted transfer documents and contract of sale for a developer in the acquisition of sixteen hotels in four states. Drafted and negotiated commercial leases for landlords. On behalf of owner, drafted and negotiated construction contracts, construction management agreements and architect's agreements. Drafted partnership agreements, contribution agreements and supporting collateral agreements for low-income housing tax credit deals.

ZEICHNER ELLMAN & KRAUSE   New York, New York
Associate, Real Estate Department   *March 1993 - August 1993*
Represented lenders in commercial and residential mortgage transactions; prepared loan documents and reviewed title. Counseled lenders in connection with federal and state lending regulatory requirements.

TWOHY, KELLEHER & GALLAGHER   *Brooklyn, New York*
Associate   *September 1991 - March 1993*
Represented lenders in restructuring distressed secured and unsecured commercial loans and sale/leaseback transactions. Represented European companies in products liability matters. Represented lenders in bankruptcy proceedings. Negotiated and closed commercial building and residential loans for lenders. Negotiated and conducted purchases, sales and refinances for corporate and individual clients. Represented twenty clients in preparation of will and trust agreements. Represented in excess of thirty estates in probate and administration proceedings.

WHITE & CASE   New York, New York
Law Clerk, Tax Department   *1989-1991*
Researched ERISA and corporate tax issues. Assisted in drafting qualified and non-qualified benefit plans.

FRIED, FRANK, HARRIS, SHRIVER   New York, New York
& JACOBSON   *1987-1988*
Legal Assistant, Litigation Department

EDUCATION:

BOSTON UNIVERSITY SCHOOL OF LAW
J.D., May 1991
  Law Journal, Staff Member

HARVARD UNIVERSITY
A.B. in English Literature, May 1988

PROFESSIONAL AFFILIATIONS:
New York State Bar Association, American Bar Association, Bar Association of the City of New York

OTHER ORGANIZATIONS:
The Peter Turner Society of Catholic Charities of the Diocese of Brooklyn and Queens

NAME
ADDRESS
TELEPHONE NUMBER

PROFESSIONAL EXPERIENCE:

CORPORATE/REAL ESTATE PRACTICE:
Drafting of agreements for the acquisition and disposition of commercially developed properties and undeveloped land by entities including Real Estate Investment Trusts; negotiation, drafting and review of leases of commercial space, representation of major institutional lender; drafting, negotiation and review of a wide range of real property instruments (including partnership, corporate, trust, joint venture and other agreements for programs of real estate ownership and offering to prospective buyers); drafting of corporate instruments (including stock transfers, resolutions and shareholder agreements) and supervision of due diligence investigations.

SPECIFIC DUTIES:

Organize and supervise the documentation, negotiations and closings of a portfolio of properties for a major pension trust; draft and organize a file of real estate/ corporate forms for boilerplate use; manage the firm escrow fund for real estate transactions (including procedures for withdrawals and I.R.S. reporting requirements); oversee all residential real estate transactions.

LEGAL EMPLOYMENT:

DEWEY BALLANTINE, New York, NY (September 1983 to Present)
Real Estate Senior Attorney

ROPES & GRAY, Boston, MA (September 1980-83)
Real Estate Associate

EDUCATION:

BOSTON UNIVERSITY SCHOOL OF LAW, Boston, MA
J.D., 1980

COLLEGE OF NEW ROCHELLE, New Rochelle, NY
A.B., History, 1977

BAR ADMISSIONS:

STATE BAR OF NEW YORK, 1981
STATE BAR OF MASSACHUSETTS, 1981

Address
Phone #

EXPERIENCE:

FIRST FIDELITY BANCORPORATION, NEWARK, NEW JERSEY
Counsel, Legal Department, Litigation & Asset Recovery Practice Group, 1994 to Present
Provide legal advice and guidance to Bank officers with respect to offensive and defensive litigation, including commercial litigation, employment law and securities law issues. Assist Bank officers with preparation of documents (including drafting forbearance agreements, loan modification documents, and assignment agreements), development of pre-litigation strategy and retention of outside counsel. Review and comment on outside counsel work product and analyze bills for legal services rendered; file responsive papers and pleadings with courts, arbitrators, and administrative agencies.

MILBANK, TWEED, HADLEY & MCCLOY, NEW YORK, NEW YORK
Associate, 1987 to 1994
Represent Institutional Lenders, Lessors, Purchasers, Other Creditors, Debtors and Trustees in Bankruptcy Litigation and Restructuring scenarios, including appearances in Bankruptcy courts on: cash collateral, relief from stay, postpetition financing, asset sale, settlement approval and other motions; fee application hearings; and pre-trial conferences. Researched and drafted motions, memoranda of law, disclosure statements and Chapter 11 plans. Supervised junior associates. Assisted John J. Jerome in drafting his Senate Testimony regarding the Swap Agreement Amendments to the Bankruptcy Code.

UNITED STATES BANKRUPTCY COURT FOR THE S.D.N.Y
Law Clerk for The Honorable Howard C. Buschman III, 1986 to 1987
Researched and drafted proposed opinions involving bankruptcy and other law in such cases as Wedtech, Prudential Lines, and Beker Industries. Assisted Judge in Court, observed trials, reviewed trial transcripts and drafted proposed findings of fact and conclusions of law.

MILBANK, TWEED, HADLEY & MCCLOY, NEW YORK, NEW YORK
Summer Associate, 1985
Banking, Bankruptcy & Corporate Rotations.

EDUCATION:

FORDHAM UNIVERSITY SCHOOL OF LAW
Juris Doctor, June 1986
Fordham Urban Law Journal, **Managing Editor,** Volume XIV

STATE UNIVERSITY OF NEW YORK AT BUFFALO SCHOOL OF MANAGEMENT
Bachelor of Science, **summa cum laude**, June 1983

ADMISSIONS:

New Jersey and New York State Bars; Federal Bar in the District of New Jersey, and the Southern and Eastern Districts of New York.

PUBLICATIONS:

Aronzon, Joyce & Moser, <u>The LTV Risk: Participants in Debt-for-Debt Exchange Transactions May Have a Smaller Bankruptcy Claim After the Exchange</u>, March 14, 1990, distributed at 1990 Spring Meeting of the ABA Section of Business Law at Boston, Massachusetts.

Buschman & Joyce, <u>The Impact of the Bankruptcy Code on Environmental Disputes</u>, 12 ALI-ABA Course Materials Journal 87 (Oct. 1987).

Home: Office:

SUMMARY OF EXPERIENCE

Twenty years as a corporate counsel with a broad range of experience in mergers and acquisitions, antitrust, commercial contracts, corporate law, SEC, financings, real estate, creditors' rights, environmental, intellectual property and regulatory law.

EXPERIENCE

INTERNATIONAL BUSINESS COMPANY   **1990 to Present**
Senior Counsel, Mergers & Acquisitions, Divestment and Diversified Businesses
Responsible for the legal work of this Fortune 50 company's acquisitions and divestment. Provide legal advice to company's diversified businesses, consisting of various non-forest product divisions and subsidiaries.
Accomplishments:
- Completed several successful multi-million dollar acquisitions and divestment.

WARING CHEMICALS, INC.   **1987 - 1990**
Assistant General Counsel
Provided legal advice and services to headquarters management and staff and divisional personnel. Supervised intellectual property and litigation outside counsel, as well as corporate and intellectual property paralegals. Performed acquisition and divestment work.
Accomplishments:
- Completed three multi-million dollar acquisitions and one multi-million dollar divestment.
- Supervised divestment of various parcels of excess real estate owned by the company.
- Supervised the successful defense of major product liability and contractual litigation.

NBF, INC.   **1981 - 1987**
Assistant General Counsel
Directed the legal affairs of headquarters and three major subsidiaries with annual sales of $4 billion. Acted as Corporate Secretary for NBF Inc. and thirty domestic and international subsidiaries.
Accomplishments:
- Negotiated and completed several multi-million dollar acquisitions.
- Managed due diligence investigation involved in half billion dollar acquisition of company.
- Established several forms of commercial contracts in the wholesaling and distribution businesses, including sales, purchase, distributorship, exchange and tolling agreements.
- Successfully defended NBF, Inc. in investigations by the U.S. Department of Customs and Bureau of Alcohol, Tobacco and Firearms.
- Negotiated and completed leasing and subleasing of various corporate and residential properties.

CORPCO, INC.   **1976 - 1981**
Attorney
Negotiated and completed acquisition and divestment agreements, performed antitrust analyses, prepared and filed SEC registration statements, and drafted and negotiated commercial contracts.
   Accomplishments:
   ▪ Negotiated and completed the acquisition of two companies, a restaurant chain and a home improvement company, with assets totaling $120 million.
   ▪ Conducted the response to a U.S. Justice Department antitrust investigation.

EDUCATION

NEW YORK UNIVERSITY SCHOOL OF LAW
LL.M. Taxation 1981

UNIVERSITY OF VIRGINIA SCHOOL OF LAW
J.D. 1976
   Member, Law Review

**CORNELL UNIVERSITY SCHOOL OF INDUSTRIAL &
LABOR RELATIONS**
B.S., 1973
   Dean's List - Three Years

PROFESSIONAL ASSOCIATIONS

Admitted to the New York State Bar and Federal Bar in the Southern and Eastern
   Districts of New York; admitted to the State Bar of Virginia.

Member, New York State Bar Association,
   Corporate Counsel and Sports and Entertainment Sections
Member, American Bar Association
Member, Corporate Bar Association

REFERENCES AVAILABLE UPON REQUEST

NAME
ADDRESS
TELEPHONE NUMBER

EXPERIENCE:

COMMUNITY SERVICE SOCIETY OF NEW YORK, INC., NEW YORK, NY

Staff Attorney (January, 1992 - Present)
Litigate cases on behalf of the economically disadvantaged in the areas of health and environmental justice. Provide legal counsel to the corporation.

Director of Health Advocacy (February, 1990 - December, 1991)
Monitored city, state and federal health legislation, regulations and policies relevant to the corporation's health agenda. Drafted legislation, testimony and memoranda advocating the health agenda.

CITY UNIVERSITY OF NEW YORK, NEW YORK, NY
JOHN JAY SCHOOL OF CRIMINAL JUSTICE
Adjunct Professor (September, 1991 - May, 1993)
Taught upper-level civil rights and criminal justice law courses with focus on the Latino experience in these areas.

NEW YORK CITY COMMISSION ON HUMAN RIGHTS, NEW YORK, NY
Attorney Trainee (October, 1987 - February, 1990)
Mediated and prosecuted discrimination complaints. Conducted training workshops for city employees and community organizations on New York City's Human Rights Law.

EAST HARLEM COLLEGE & CAREER COUNSELING PROGRAM, INC., NEW YORK, NY
Executive Director (June, 1980 - June, 1985)
Chief Executive Officer responsible for policy development and implementation, fiscal decisions and development activities including writing grant proposals.

EDUCATION:

COLUMBIA UNIVERSITY SCHOOL OF LAW
J.D., 1987

NEW YORK UNIVERSITY
M.P.A., 1984

LEMOYNE COLLEGE
B.A., 1977

BAR ADMISSIONS:

U.S. District Court for the Eastern District, New York State Court

NAME

Address   Phone

PROFILE:

Practicing attorney in litigation and employment law with experience managing human resources for a public relations firm. Combines excellent oral and written communication skills with ability to inspire client and colleague confidence. Accomplished speaker with energetic personality.

EXPERIENCE:

MANNING, SELVAGE & LEE, Public Relations, New York, NY
Senior Vice President, Director of Human Resources, 1993-1994
Responsible for all human resource and benefit functions for 200-person firm with five offices in the United States.

- Interpreted all employee policies and issued written communications regarding same, as well as benefit developments. Standardized medical leave policy in cases of pregnancy-related disabilities, which clarified policy and reduced potential for liability.
- Revised employee handbook, guidelines for entry-level employees and affirmative action plans.
- Negotiated employment contracts of managing directors in U.K. office.
- Formulated 1994 department budgets for staffing, training, travel and entertainment.
- Conducted heavy recruiting to fill exempt and non-exempt positions at all levels. Established a method of recruitment, orientation and training for largest staff increase in two years in New York.
- Initiated diversity hiring and recruitment program, achieving goal in New York within six weeks.
- Prepared compensation analysis and recommended employees for participation in special salary adjustment pool.
- Implemented open enrollment process for new 1994 flexible benefits program.

DAVIS & GILBERT, New York, NY
Associate (Employment Law/Commercial Litigation), 1989-1993

- Represented employers in employment discrimination and other commercial litigation.
- Advised clients on issues involving federal, state and local fair employment and anti-discrimination laws.
- Conducted investigations into charges brought at EEOC and state and city fair employment agencies, and drafted position statements denying these charges. Received favorable rulings on all but one of more than 20 charges.
- Wrote employee policies and documents relating to hiring and termination, such as offer letters, severance agreements, ADEA and other releases and promissory notes.
- Appeared in federal and state court, New York State's Division of Human Rights and Department of Labor (Unemployment Insurance Division) and Criminal Court. Conducted or defended more than 25 depositions.
- Drafted motion papers, pleadings, legal memoranda, discovery requests and responses, jury charges and other trial documents.
- Second-chaired two ADEA jury trials in Southern District of New York and a mediation in Texas.
- Initiated ERISA proceeding on behalf of plaintiffs which went from complaint through summary judgment to resolution within 18 months and established new law in the Second Circuit.

SEWARD & KISSEL, New York, NY
Associate (Commercial Litigation), 1987-1989
- Research, writing, document review and trial preparation in employment discrimination and other litigation.

PUBLICATION AND AWARDS:

- Note, compelled Waiver of Bank Secrecy in the Cayman Islands: Solution to International Tax Evasion or Threat to Sovereignty of Nations?, 9 Fordham Int'l L.J.7\680 (1986).
- 1986 Francis O. Deak Award: awarded by American Society of International Law and Association of Student International Law Societies to outstanding student writing in international law.
- 1987 Edgar Ansel Mowrer Memorial Award: awarded at graduation by Umano Foundation to best paper on international law.
- Bay v. Times Mirror Magazines: Two Important Lessons About Defending Age Discrimination Claims, D&G Digest (Davis & Gilbert Client Newsletter), July 1992 (Part I) and September 1992 (Part II) (co-authored with Howard J. Rubin, Esq.)
- Hiring & Firing the Older Employee, Gear Technology (The Journal of Gear Manufacturing), January/February 1993 (co-authored as above)
- Severance and Releases: Avoiding Lawsuits from Employee terminations, D&G Digest, September/October 1993 (co-authored as above).

EDUCATION:
FORDHAM UNIVERSITY SCHOOL OF LAW, J.D., 1987
- Articles Editor, Fordham International Law Journal
- Research Assistant, Professor Barry E. Hawk
- Teaching Assistant, First-Year Legal Writing

MOUNT HOLYOKE COLLEGE, A.B., American Studies, 1984
- Concentration in theater. Appeared in mainstage and student productions.

OFFICES:
The University Club, New York, New York
- Member, Annual Events Committee, 1993 to present
- Member, Planning Committee, Subcommittee on Women Members, 1992 to present

Fordham International Law Journal Alumni Association, Inc.
- President, 1990-1994; Treasurer, 1988-1990
- Managing Editor and contributing writer, Association newsletter, 1992 to present

Mount Holyoke College
- Class Agent, 1989-1994

Fordham University School of Law
- Chairperson, Fifth Reunion Committee, 1992

BAR ADMISSIONS:
New York, S.D.N.Y., E.D.N.Y. (1988); Connecticut (1987); U.S. Supreme Court (1992)

AFFILIATIONS:
- American Bar Association, Section on Labor and Employment Law
- Toastmasters International: working towards CTM certificate
- Volunteer Lawyers for the Arts

MISCELLANEOUS:
Featured speaker, "The Joan Hamburg Show," WOR Radio panel on Career Transitions.

Appendix B

RECOMMENDED READING

Altman, Mary Ann, *Life After Law: Second Careers for Lawyers*, The Wayne Smith Company, Inc., (1991).

Anderson, Nancy, *Work With Passion*, Carroll & Graf and Whatever Publishing (1984).

Armstrong, Howard, *High Impact Telephone Networking for Job Hunters*, Bob Adams, Inc., Holbrook, MA (1992).

Arron, Deborah L., *What Can You Do With a Law Degree?* Niche Press, Seattle, WA (1992).

Barber, Professor David H., *Surviving Your Role As a Lawyer*, Spectra Publishing Co., Inc., Dillon, CO (1987).

Bellon, Lee Ann, "Coping with Job-Loss Trauma," *The National Law Journal*, (November 1991).

Birsner, E. Patricia, *The 40+ Job Hunting Guide*, Facts on File, New York, NY (1991).

Bolles, Richard N., *What Color is Your Parachute?*, Ten Speed Press, Berkeley, CA (1996).

Byers, Mark, Don Samuelson, Gordon Williamson, *Lawyers in Transition: Planning a Life in the Law*, The Barkley Company, Inc., Natick, MA (1988).

Cain, George. H; *Turning Points: New Paths and Second Careers For Lawyers*, American Bar Association, Chicago, IL (1994)

Carey, Williams T., *Law Students: How to Get a Job When There Aren't Any*, Carolina Academic Press, Durham, NC (1986).

Catalyst Staff, *What to Do With the Rest of Your Life*, Simon & Schuster, New York, NY (1980).

Catalyst Staff, *Marketing Yourself*, Bantam Books New York, NY (1980).

Chin-Lee, Cynthia, *It's Who You Know—Career Strategies for Making Effective Personal Contacts*, Pfeiffer and Co. (1993).

Crystal, John C. and Richard N. Bolles, *Where Do I Go From Here With My Life?*, Ten Speed Press, Berkley, CA (1974).

Federal Reports, *JD Preferred: 400+ Things You Can Do With a Law Degree (Other than Practice Law)*, Federal Reports, Inc., Washington, DC (1994).

Fournier, Myra and Spin, Jeffrey, *Encyclopedia of Job Winning Resumes*, Round Lake Publishing, Ridgefield, CT (1993).

Good, C. Edward, *Does Your Resume Wear Blue Jeans?*, Word Store, Charlottesville, VA, (1985).

Graham, Lawrence Otis, *The Best Companies for Minorities*, Penguin Books, New York, NY (1993).

Granfield, Robert, *Making Elite Lawyers—Vision of Law at Harvard and Beyond*, Routledge, New York, NY (1992).

Grant, Kathleen and Werner, Wendy, *The Road Not Taken: Job Seekers Excerpt*, The National Association for Law Placement, Washington, DC (1991).

Harkavy, Michael, *101 Careers: A Guide to the Fastest—Growing Opportunities*, Wiley, New York, NY (1990).

Jackson, Tom, *Guerilla Tactics in the New Job Market*, Bantam, New York, NY (1991).

Kennedy, Joyce Lain, *Electronic Job Search Revolution*, Wiley, New York, NY (1994).

Killoughey, D.M. (Editor), *Breaking Traditions: Work Alternatives for Lawyers*, Section of Law Practice Management, American Bar Association (1993).

Koltnow, Emily and Dumas, Lynne S., *Congratulations! You've Been Fired*, Ballantine Books, New York, NY (1990).

Krannich, Ronald L. and Caryl Rae Krannich, *Dynamite Salary Negotiations*, Impact Publications, Manassas Park, VA (1993).

Krannich, Ronald L. and Caryl Rae Krannich, *The New Network Your Way to Job and Career Success*, Impact Publications, Manassas Park, VA (1993).

Krannich, Ronald L., *Change Your Job, Change Your Life*, Impact Publications, Manassas Park, VA (1995).

Krannich, Ronald L. and Caryl Rae Krannich, *The Almanac of American Government Jobs and Careers*, Impact Publications, Manassas Park, VA (1991).

Krannich, Ronald L. and Caryl Rae Krannich, *Jobs and Careers With Nonprofit Organizations*, Impact Publications, Manassas Park, VA (1996).

Krannich, Ronald L. and Caryl Rae Krannich, *The Complete Guide to Public Employment*, Impact Publications, Manassas Park, VA (1994).

Lewis, Adele, *How to Write Better Resumes*, Barron's Educational Series, Inc., Woodbury, New York (1983).

McNeil, Heidi L. (Editor), *Changing Jobs: A Handbook for Lawyers for the 1990's*, American Bar Association, Chicago, IL (1994).

Magness, Michael K., "The Art of Effective Interviewing," *National Law Journal*, P. 15, (October 11, 1982).

Mandell, Terri, *Power Shmoozing: The Etiquette for Social and Business Success*, First House Press, Los Angeles, CA (1993).

Moll, Richard W., *The Lure of the Law—Why People Become Lawyers, and What the Profession Does to Them*, Penguin Books, New York, NY (1990).

Myers, Isabel B; with Peter B. Myers, *Gifts Differing*, Consulting Psychologists Press, Palo Alto, CA (1980).

National Association for Law Placement, *Employment Report and Salary Survey*, NALP, Washington, DC (Published Anually).

National Association for Law Placement, *Guide to Small Firm Employment*, NALP, Washington, DC (1992).

National Association for Law Placement, *Profiles of Minority Attorneys in Specialty Practices*, NALP, Washington, DC (1995).

Petras, Kathryn and Ross, *The Over 40 Job Guide*, Simon and Schuster, New York, NY (1993).

Raelin, Joseph A., *The Salaried Professional: How to Make the Most of Your Career*, Praeger Publishers, New York, NY (1984).

Ray, Samuel, *Resumes for the Over 50 Job Hunter*, Wiley, New York, NY (1993).

Richard, L.R., "Resolving for New Year to Effectively Plan Career," *Pennsylvania Law Journal-Reporter*, p.4, Col. 1 (January 21, 1991).

Richard, L.R., "Understanding Lawyers Personalities," *The Pennsylvania Lawyer*, pp. 14(2), 22-26, 32 (1992).

Richard, L.R., "Lawyer Dissatisfaction Rising, But Many Alternatives Exist" *Pennsylvania Law Journal-Reporter*, p. 4,8 (November 5, 1990).

Richard, L.R., "Personality Styles of U.S. Lawyers: New Findings," *ABA Journal* (July 1993).

Rodin, Robert J., *Full Potential: Your Career and Life Planning Workbook*, McGraw-Hill, New York, NY (1983).

Rossman, Marge, *When the Headhunter Calls*, Contemporary Books, Inc., Chicago, IL (1981).

Sher, Barbara, *Wishcraft: How to Get What You Really Want*, Ballantine Books, New York, NY (1979).

Sher, Barbara, *I Could Do Anything If Only I Knew What It Was*, Delacorte Press, New York, NY (1994).

Sinetar, Marsha, *Do What You Love, The Money Will Follow*, Paulist Press, New York, NY (1987).

Smith, Russell, Dr., *The Right SF 171 Writer*, Impact Publications, Manassas Park, VA (1994).

Sturman, Gerald, M., *If You Knew Who You Were, You Could Be Who You Are*, Bierman House, Woodstock, NY (1989).

Thorner, Abbie W., *Now Hiring: Government Jobs for Lawyers*, Law Student Division, American Bar Association, Chicago, IL (1990).

Utley, Frances, *Nonlegal Careers for Lawyers in the Private Sector*, American Bar Association, Chicago, IL (1984).

Walton, Kimm A., *Guerilla Tactics for Getting the Legal Job of Your Dreams*, Harcourt Brace, Chicago, IL (1995).

Wasserman, Steven and J.W. O'Brien, *Law and Legal Information Directory*, 4th Edition, Gale Research Co., Detroit, MI (1986).

Wayne, Ellen and Betsy McCombs, *Legal Careers—Choices and Options*, Vol.1, NALP, Washington, DC (1983).

Wendleton, Kate, *Through the Brick Wall: How to Job Hunt in a Tight Market*, Villard, New York, NY (1992).

Zemans, Frances Kahn and Victor G. Rosenblum, *The Making of a Public Profession*, American Bar Foundation, Chicago, IL (1981).

INDEX

ABOUT THE AUTHORS

Kathleen Brady

Kathleen Brady, Assistant Dean of Fordham University School of Law's Career Planning Center and the 1995-96 President of the National Association for Law Placement (NALP), has been involved with career planning and placement for lawyers since 1986. Additionally, Kathleen is a member of two committees at the Association of the Bar for the City of New York: The Recruitment and Retention of Lawyers and Lawyers in Transition.

A frequent speaker for the National Association for Law Placement, the Association of the Bar for the City of New York and the New York Country Lawyers Association, Ms. Brady has covered topics including Counseling Alumni, Career Planning for the Experienced Attorney, Networking Strategies, Interviewing Techniques, Recovering from a Layoff, Improving Employment Opportunities for Students and Graduates, Job Hunting over 40, How to Work a Room, and Alternative Careers for Lawyers.

She has published two articles in the New York Law Journal entitled "A Plan for Tackling the Legal Job Search" and "Networking Can Uncover Opportunities" as well as chapters in *Changing Jobs: A Handbook for Lawyers*, published by the A.B.A. Young Lawyers Division and *Law School Guide to Public Interest Careers - Counseling Students not Participating in OCI*, published by the National Association for Law Placement.

Upon graduating Fordham College, Ms. Brady served as a volunteer with the Jesuit Volunteer Corps in Los Angeles working with youthful offenders. She has done graduate work at New York University School of Social Work and at Fordham University Graduate School of Education.

Hillary Jayne Mantis

Hillary Jayne Mantis, Esq., is Director of the Career Planning Center at Fordham University School of Law. Prior to joining the staff of Fordham, she was Associate Director of Career Services at New York Law School. She is a graduate of Brown University and Boston College Law School. Her recruitment and counseling activities have included specialized work in the areas of alternative legal careers, public interest employment and alumni career counseling.

Ms. Mantis served as Chair of the American Bar Association Young Lawyers Division Career Issues Committee in 1993-94. In addition, she has been Chair of the New York County Lawyers' Association Committee on Lawyer Placement, Subcommittee Chair of the Association of the Bar of the City of New York's special Committee on Law Student Perspectives, and served as the National Association for Law Placement's Liaison to the A.B.A. Section on Law Practice Management. She is currently on the editorial board of the American Bar Association's *Barrister Magazine*.

Ms. Mantis has spoken and conducted many programs at Fordham University Law School, New York Law School, the New York City Bar Association, the New York County Lawyers' Association and the American Bar Association. She has published several articles on career development in publications including *The New York Law Journal*, and the *National Association for Law Placement Annual Review*. She has written a chapter in *Breaking Traditions: Work Alternatives for Lawyers*, published by the Law Practice Management Section of the A.B.A., and has written a chapter and served as contributing editor of *Changing Jobs: A Handbook for Lawyers in the 90's*, published by the A.B.A. Young Lawyers Division. She writes a regular career column, *Career Notes*, for the New York County Lawyer's Association Bulletin. Prior to joining the staff of New York Law School, she was involved in politics and public interest law.

CAREER RESOURCES

Contact Impact Publications to receive a free copy of their latest comprehensive and annotated catalog of career resources (hundreds of books, directories, subscriptions, training programs, audiocassettes, videos, computer software programs, multimedia, and CD-ROM).

The following career resources are available from Impact Publications. Complete the following form or list the titles, include shipping (see the formula at the end), enclose payment, and send your order to:

IMPACT PUBLICATIONS
9104-N Manassas Drive
Manassas Park, VA 22111-5211
Tel. 703/361-7300 or Fax 703/335-9486

Orders from individuals must be prepaid by check, moneyorder, Visa, MasterCard, or American Express number. We accept telephone and fax orders with a credit card number.

Qty.	TITLES	Price	TOTAL

JOBS FOR LAWYERS

Qty.	TITLES	Price	TOTAL
__	Best Resumes for Attorneys	$14.95	____
__	Careers in Law	$16.95	____
__	Job Search '96—Clerkship Edition (software)	$129.00	____
__	Job Search '96—Law Firm Edition (software)	$99.00	____
__	Jobs for Lawyers	$14.95	____

INTERVIEWS & SALARY NEGOTIATIONS

___ 60 Seconds and You're Hired!	$ 9.95	_____
___ 101 Questions to Ask At Your Job Interview	$14.95	_____
___ Conquer Interview Objections	$10.95	_____
___ Dynamite Answers to Interview Questions	$11.95	_____
___ Dynamite Salary Negotiation	$12.95	_____
___ Interview for Success	$13.95	_____
___ Interview Power	$12.95	_____
___ Naked At the Interview	$10.95	_____
___ Perfect Interview	$17.95	_____
___ Power Interviews	$12.95	_____
___ Sweaty Palms	$8.95	_____

DRESS, APPEARANCE, IMAGE

___ 110 Mistakes Working Women Make/Dressing Smart	$9.95	_____
___ John Molloy's New Dress for Success	$10.95	_____
___ Red Socks Don't Work! (Men's Clothing)	$14.95	_____

RESUMES, LETTERS, & NETWORKING

___ Dynamite Cover Letters	$11.95	_____
___ Dynamite Resumes	$11.95	_____
___ Electronic Resumes for the New Job Market	$11.95	_____
___ Great Connections	$11.95	_____
___ High Impact Resumes and Letters	$14.95	_____
___ How to Work a Room	$9.95	_____
___ Job Search Letters That Get Results	$15.95	_____
___ New Network Your Way to Job and Career Success	$15.95	_____

JOB SEARCH STRATEGIES AND TACTICS

___ Change Your Job, Change Your Life	$15.95	_____
___ Complete Job Finder's Guide to the 90's	$13.95	_____
___ Dynamite Tele-Search	$12.95	_____
___ Five Secrets to Finding a Job	$12.95	_____
___ How to Get Interviews From Classified Job Ads	$14.95	_____
___ How to Succeed Without a Career Path	$13.95	_____
___ Rites of Passage at $100,000+	$29.95	_____
___ Ultimate Job Source CD-ROM	$49.95	_____
___ What Color Is Your Parachute?	$14.95	_____

BEST JOBS AND EMPLOYERS FOR THE 90's

___ 100 Best Companies to Work for in America	$27.95	_____
___ 100 Best Jobs for the 1990s and Beyond	$19.95	_____
___ 101 Careers	$14.95	_____
___ 150 Companies for Liberal Arts Graduates	$12.95	_____
___ Adams Jobs Almanac 1996	$15.00	_____
___ American Almanac of Jobs and Salaries	$17.00	_____

___ America's Fastest Growing Employers $15.95 _____
___ Best Jobs for the 1990s and Into the 21st Century $19.95 _____
___ Careers Encyclopedia $39.95 _____
___ Companies That Care $12.95 _____
___ Great Place to Work $9.95 _____
___ Hoover's Guide to Computer Companies (with disk) $34.95 _____
___ Hoover's Masterlist of 2,500 of America's
Largest and Fastest Growing Employers (with disk) $19.95 _____
___ Job Seeker's Guide to 1000 Top Employers $22.95 _____
___ Jobs 1996 $15.00 _____
___ Jobs Rated Almanac $16.95 _____
___ New Emerging Careers $14.95 _____
___ Quantum Companies $21.95 _____
___ Top Professions $10.95 _____

ALTERNATIVE JOBS AND CAREERS

___ Advertising Career Directory $17.95 _____
___ Business and Finance Career Directory $17.95 _____
___ But What If I Don't Want to Go to College? $10.95 _____
___ Career Opportunities in Art $29.95 _____
___ Career Opportunities in Music Industry $29.95 _____
___ Career Opportunities in the Sports Industry $29.95 _____
___ Career Opportunities in Television, Cable, and Video $29.95 _____
___ Career Opportunities in Theater and Performing Arts $29.95 _____
___ Career Opportunities in Writing $29.95 _____
___ Careers for Animal Lovers $12.95 _____
___ Careers for Bookworms $12.95 _____
___ Careers for Computer Buffs $12.95 _____
___ Careers for Craft People $12.95 _____
___ Careers for Culture Lovers $12.95 _____
___ Careers for Environmental Types $12.95 _____
___ Careers for Foreign Language Aficionados $12.95 _____
___ Careers for Good Samaritans $12.95 _____
___ Careers for Gourmets $12.95 _____
___ Careers for History Buffs $12.95 _____
___ Careers for Kids at Heart $12.95 _____
___ Careers for Nature Lovers $12.95 _____
___ Careers for Night Owls $12.95 _____
___ Careers for Number Crunchers $12.95 _____
___ Careers for Shutterbugs $12.95 _____
___ Careers for Sports Nuts $12.95 _____
___ Careers for Travel Buffs $12.95 _____
___ Careers in Accounting $16.95 _____
___ Careers in Advertising $16.95 _____
___ Careers in Business $16.95 _____
___ Careers in Child Care $16.95 _____
___ Careers in Communications $16.95 _____
___ Careers in Computers $16.95 _____
___ Careers in Education $16.95 _____
___ Careers in Engineering $16.95 _____
___ Careers in Finance $16.95 _____
___ Careers in Government $16.95 _____

___ Careers in Health Care	$16.95	_____
___ Careers in High Tech	$16.95	_____
___ Careers in Journalism	$16.95	_____
___ Careers in Marketing	$16.95	_____
___ Careers in Medicine	$16.95	_____
___ Careers in Science	$16.95	_____
___ Careers in Social and Rehabilitation Services	$16.95	_____
___ Environmental Career Directory	$17.95	_____
___ Job Opps in Business	$19.95	_____
___ Job Opps in Engineering and Technology	$19.95	_____
___ Job Opps in Health Care	$19.95	_____
___ Jobs for People Who Love Computers and the the Information Highway	$13.95	_____
___ Jobs for People Who Love Hotels, Resorts, and Cruise Ships	$13.95	_____
___ Jobs for People Who Love Health Care and Nursing	$13.95	_____
___ Jobs for People Who Love to Work From Home	$13.95	_____
___ Jobs for People Who Love Travel	$15.95	_____
___ Marketing and Sales Career Directory	$17.95	_____
___ Opportunities in Advertising	$13.95	_____
___ Opportunities in Airline Careers	$13.95	_____
___ Opportunities in Banking	$13.95	_____
___ Opportunities in Broadcasting	$13.95	_____
___ Opportunities in Business Management	$13.95	_____
___ Opportunities in Child Care	$13.95	_____
___ Opportunities in Craft Careers	$13.95	_____
___ Opportunities in Electrical Trades	$13.95	_____
___ Opportunities in Eye Care	$13.95	_____
___ Opportunities in Gerontology	$13.95	_____
___ Opportunities in Interior Design	$13.95	_____
___ Opportunities in Laser Technology	$13.95	_____
___ Opportunities in Microelectronics	$13.95	_____
___ Opportunities in Nonprofit Organizations	$13.95	_____
___ Opportunities in Optometry	$13.95	_____
___ Opportunities in Pharmacy	$13.95	_____
___ Opportunities in Psychology	$13.95	_____
___ Opportunities in Public Relations	$13.95	_____
___ Opportunities in Robotics	$13.95	_____
___ Opportunities in Sports and Athletics	$13.95	_____
___ Opportunities in Sports Medicine	$13.95	_____
___ Opportunities in Telecommunications	$13.95	_____
___ Opportunities in Transportation	$13.95	_____
___ Opportunities in Trucking	$13.95	_____
___ Opportunities in Waste Management	$13.95	_____
___ Outdoor Careers	$14.95	_____
___ Radio and Television Career Directory	$17.95	_____
___ Travel and Hospitality Career Directory	$17.95	_____

KEY DIRECTORIES

___ American Salaries and Wages Survey	$115.00	_____
___ Career Training Sourcebook	$24.95	_____
___ Careers Encyclopedia	$39.95	_____

___ Dictionary of Occupational Titles $39.95 _____
___ Directory of Executive Recruiters $44.95 _____
___ Encyclopedia of Associations $1,160.00 _____
___ Encyclopedia of Careers & Vocational Guidance $129.95 _____
___ Hoover's American Business $29.95 _____
___ Hoover's World Business $27.95 _____
___ Internships 1996 $21.95 _____
___ Job Bank Guide to Employment Services $149.95 _____
___ Job Hunter's Sourcebook $69.95 _____
___ Moving and Relocation Directory $179.95 _____
___ National Fax Directory $99.00 _____
___ National Job Bank $249.95 _____
___ National Trade and Professional Associations $79.95 _____
___ Occupational Outlook Handbook $21.95 _____
___ Personnel Executives Contactbook $149.00 _____
___ Professional Careers Sourcebook $89.95 _____
___ Vocational Careers Sourcebook $79.95 _____

TELEPHONE AND JOB HOTLINE DIRECTORIES

___ Directory of Executive Recruiters $44.95 _____
___ Government Directory of Addresses
and Telephone Numbers $149.95 _____
___ Job Hotlines USA $24.95 _____
___ Job Hunter's Yellow Pages $59.00 _____
___ National Directory of Addresses and
Telephone Numbers $99.95 _____

JOB VACANCY SOURCEBOOKS

___ Government Job Finder $16.95 _____
___ Non-Profit's Job Finder $16.95 _____
___ Professional's Private Sector Job Finder $18.95 _____

ELECTRONIC JOB SEARCH RESOURCES

___ Electronic Job Search Revolution $12.95 _____
___ Electronic Resume Revolution $12.95 _____
___ Electronic Resumes for the New Job Market $11.95 _____
___ Hook Up, Get Hired $12.95 _____
___ The Job-Seeker's Guide to On-Line Resources $14.95 _____
___ On-Line Job Search Companion $14.95 _____
___ Using the Internet in Your Job Search $16.95 _____

CITY AND STATE JOB FINDERS (Adams Media's Job Banks)

___ Atlanta $15.95 _____
___ Boston $15.95 _____
___ Chicago $15.95 _____
___ Dallas/Fort Worth $15.95 _____
___ Denver $15.95 _____
___ Florida $15.95 _____

___ Houston	$15.95	_____
___ Los Angeles	$15.95	_____
___ Minneapolis	$15.95	_____
___ New York	$15.95	_____
___ Philadelphia	$15.95	_____
___ San Francisco	$15.95	_____
___ Seattle	$15.95	_____
___ Washington, DC	$15.95	_____

CITY AND STATE JOB FINDERS (Surrey Books)

___ Atlanta	$15.95	_____
___ Boston	$15.95	_____
___ Dallas/Fort Worth	$15.95	_____
___ Houston	$15.95	_____
___ New York	$15.95	_____
___ San Francisco	$15.95	_____
___ Seattle and Portland	$15.95	_____
___ Southern California	$15.95	_____
___ Washington, DC	$15.95	_____

INTERNATIONAL, OVERSEAS, AND TRAVEL JOBS

___ Almanac of International Jobs and Careers	$19.95	_____
___ Complete Guide to International Jobs & Careers	$13.95	_____
___ Guide to Careers in World Affairs	$14.95	_____
___ How to Get a Job in Europe	$17.95	_____
___ How to Get a Job in the Pacific Rim	$17.95	_____
___ Jobs for People Who Love Travel	$15.95	_____
___ Jobs in Russia and the Newly Independent States	$15.95	_____
___ Jobs Worldwide	$17.95	_____

PUBLIC-ORIENTED CAREERS

___ Complete Guide to Public Employment	$19.95	_____
___ Directory of Federal Jobs and Employers	$21.95	_____
___ Federal Applications That Get Results	$23.95	_____
___ Federal Jobs in Computers	$14.95	_____
___ Federal Jobs in Finance and Accounting	$14.95	_____
___ Federal Jobs in Law Enforcement	$14.95	_____
___ Federal Jobs in Nursing and Health Sciences	$14.95	_____
___ Federal Jobs in Office Administration	$14.95	_____
___ Federal Jobs in Secret Operations	$14.95	_____
___ Find a Federal Job Fast!	$13.95	_____
___ Government Job Finder	$16.95	_____
___ Jobs and Careers With Nonprofit Organizations	$15.95	_____

JOB LISTINGS & VACANCY ANNOUNCEMENTS

___ Executive Recruiter News	$157.00	_____
___ Federal Career Opportunities (6 biweekly issues)	$39.00	_____
___ International Employment Gazette (6 biweekly issues)	$35.00	_____

SKILLS, TESTING, SELF-ASSESSMENT

___ Discover the Best Jobs for You	$11.95	___
___ Do What You Are	$15.95	___
___ Do What You Love, the Money Will Follow	$11.95	___
___ I Could Do Anything If I Only Know What It Was	$19.95	___
___ Where Do I Go With the Rest of My Life?	$11.95	___
___ Wishcraft	$11.95	___

MILITARY

___ From Air Force Blue to Corporate Gray	$17.95	___
___ From Army Green to Corporate Gray	$15.95	___
___ From Navy Blue to Corporate Gray	$17.95	___
___ Resumes and Cover Letters for Transitioning Military Personnel	$17.95	___

WOMEN AND SPOUSES

___ Doing It All Isn't Everything	$19.95	___
___ New Relocating Spouse's Guide to Employment	$14.95	___
___ Survival Guide for Women	$16.95	___

MINORITIES AND DISABLED

___ Best Companies for Minorities	$12.00	___
___ Big Book of Minority Opportunities	$39.95	___
___ Job Strategies for People With Disabilities	$14.95	___
___ Minority Organizations	$49.95	___

ENTREPRENEURSHIP AND SELF-EMPLOYMENT

___ 101 Best Businesses to Start	$15.00	___
___ Best Home-Based Businesses for the 90s	$12.95	___
___ Entrepreneur's Guide to Starting a Successful Business	$16.95	___

VIDEOS

___ Dialing for Jobs	$139.00	___
___ Directing Your Successful Job Search	$99.95	___
___ JobSearch—The Inside Track	$1295.00	___
___ Looking Ahead	$129.95	___
___ Winning At Job Hunting in the 90s	$89.95	___

COMPUTER SOFTWARE PROGRAMS (IBM or Compatibles)

___ Cambridge Career Counseling System	$349.00	___
___ INSTANT Job Hunting Letters	$39.95	___
___ JobHunt for Window®	$59.95	___
___ Resumemaker With Career Planning	$49.95	___
___ You're Hired!	$59.95	___

CD-ROM

___ America's Top Jobs	$295.00	_____
___ CD-ROM Version of the Occupational Outlook Handbook	$399.00	_____
___ Electronic Guide for Occupational Exploration	$295.00	_____
___ Encyclopedia of Careers and Vocational Guidance	$199.95	_____
___ Interview Skills of the Future	$199.00	_____
___ Job Search Skills of the 21st Century	$199.00	_____
___ Multimedia Career Center	$385.00	_____
___ Occupational Outlook On CD-ROM	$29.95	_____
___ Resume Revolution	$99.00	_____
___ Tech Prep Careers for the Future	$349.00	_____
___ Ultimate Job Source (Individual Version)	$49.95	_____
___ Ultimate Job Source (Professional Version with DOT)	$149.95	_____

SUBTOTAL _____

Virginia residents add 4½% sales tax _____

POSTAGE/HANDLING ($4 for first product and $1 for each additional) ___$4.00___

Number of additional titles x $1.00 ---------- _____

TOTAL ENCLOSED ----------------- _____

NAME _____

ADDRESS _____

_____

_____

❑ I enclose check/moneyorder for $ _____ made payable to IMPACT PUBLICATIONS.

❑ Please charge $ _____ to my credit card:

Card # _____

Expiration date: _____ / _____

Signature _____